VOLPONE &
THE ALCHEMIST

NOTES

including
Life and Background
Plot Summaries and Commentaries
Character Analyses
Review Questions
Special Topics

by
James P. McGlone, Ph.D.
Department of Communication Arts
Seton Hall University

and
A. M. I. Fiskin, Ph.D.
Department of English
Pennsylvania State University

consulting editor
James L. Roberts, Ph.D.
Department of English
University of Nebraska

Cliffs Notes
INCORPORATED
LINCOLN, NEBRASKA   68501

ISBN 0-8220-1349-5

© Copyright 1967

by

C. K. Hillegass

All Rights Reserved

Printed in U.S.A.

CONTENTS

LIFE AND BACKGROUND 5

"VOLPONE" 6

General Plot Summary 6

List of Characters 9

Summaries and Commentaries 11
    Act I 11
    Act II 18
    Act III 27
    Act IV 40
    Act V 49

Character Analyses 65

Review Questions 69

"THE ALCHEMIST" 71

Alchemy and Allied Arts 71

List of Characters 73

Plot Summary 75

Summaries and Commentaries 79
    Dedication 79
    To the Reader 80
    Prologue 80
    Argument 81
    Act I 81

Act II	84
Act III	88
Act IV	93
Act V	99
Characterization	105
Review Questions	108

Life and Background

Ben Jonson was born in 1572 or 1573, a month or so after his father's death. His father was a minister and his stepfather a bricklayer. Someone financed Jonson's education at Westminster School, where the historian William Camden introduced him to the classics. After a few weeks at Cambridge, Jonson was forced to take up bricklaying. Later he is found soldiering in the Netherlands, fighting a duel with an enemy soldier, killing him, and returning home with heroic tales to enlarge upon.

Swiftly, he married, begot and buried several children, fought and reconciled with his wife, and began a theatrical career. Almost at once he wrote with Thomas Nashe a play entitled *The Isle of Dogs* (1597). Both playwrights were charged with seditious and slanderous matter, but only Jonson was captured and clapped in irons. Upon release, Jonson joined Philip Henslowe's theatrical company. A year later, at the Globe theater, Jonson had his first stage success with *Every Man in His Humour*.

The Latins used the word *humour* to mean moisture or fluid; the tradition of the medical profession used the word regarding four fluids: blood, phlegm, black bile, and yellow bile. Depending on whichever of the four fluids was dominant, the person possessed of the humour was said to be sanguine, phlegmatic, melancholic, or choleric.

The popularity of this "play of humours" caused Jonson to leave acting for writing. He collaborated on court masques with the famed scene designer Inigo Jones, enjoying much success. But his hot temper found him an argument which precipitated a duel with the actor Gabriel Spencer. He killed his opponent and was jailed for murder (1598). Jonson eventually won his release, pleading benefit of clergy because he could read the Latin Psalter like a clerk, but not without punishment: the letter *T* was branded on his thumb. Later, after two more comedies, he was satirized by another playwright, Thomas Dekker, in *Satiromastix*, which called him puny, pockmarked, conceited pedant, murderer, and bricklayer. Undaunted, Jonson turned out the static and moralistic *Sejanus*, which flopped on the stage but won him the support of Lord Aubigny upon publication.

Jonson collaborated on *Eastward Ho!*, which insulted the Scots and the king, and placed the authors behind bars. In 1606, *Volpone* put its author at the top on London's comic stage. In 1610, *The Alchemist* appeared and in 1614 the attack on London Puritans, *Bartholomew Fair*. These plays cemented Jonson's reputation as the great poet of English comedy. He received subsidies from the Crown for his work and continued to write court masques until a quarrel with Jones returned him to full-time work in the commercial theater.

Jonson gathered many young poets and playwrights around him, and they were eventually called the "Tribe of Ben." Among their number could be included James Shirley, Thomas Carew, and Robert Herrick.

Ben Jonson was never a provident man. By 1629, he lived alone, bedridden with paralysis and without funds. After eight years of pain and penury, he died and was buried in Westminster Abbey (1637). Jonson's great critic and editor, C. H. Herford, thought the playwright was powerful but without charm; Jonson seemed impressive, though he was unattractive to posterity. At any rate, Jonson possessed a belligerent and quarrelsome personality, but he was a faithful friend, fearless, and intellectually honest. One of his contemporaries summed up his person for the epitaph on his tomb in Westminster Abbey: "O Rare Ben Jonson."

Volpone Notes

GENERAL PLOT SUMMARY

Volpone, a Venetian nobleman, has no relative to make his heir; he must name someone his beneficiary. Several rivals try to attain his favor by bringing the sick Volpone gifts that they hope will be returned tenfold. Mosca, a clever parasite to Volpone, encourages the three major gulls to give until it hurts. These birds of prey are Voltore, a lawyer; Corbaccio, an old miser about to die himself; Corvino, a rich merchant and husband to Celia, a beautiful lady of Venice. Also naively competing for Volpone's wealth is Lady Would-be, the affected wife of an English knight, Sir Politic Would-be. After each gull is fleeced before our eyes, Mosca encourages Volpone to think of seeking a greater treasure than gold: the wife of Corvino. After a sensuous description by Mosca, Volpone resolves to see this paragon of beauty.

As the second act begins, Volpone appears beneath Celia's window disguised as a mountebank. Jealous Corvino drives him away upon discovering his wife in an upper window. While Corvino threatens his wife with closer incarceration, Volpone sings to Mosca of her beauty and his desire. Mosca hatches a plot to secure Celia for his master. He tells Corvino that the mountebank's oil, purchased for Volpone by Corbaccio, has revived the flagging health of the fox. However, if Volpone is to live on, he must sleep with some young woman. The others are seeking the cure for Volpone, and Corvino must hurry or lose his investment. Corvino wisely suggests a courtesan, but Mosca slyly rejects this plan, reasoning that an artful quean might cheat them all. Finally, Corvino offers his wife. He is convinced that she is safe, and Mosca is sent to tell Volpone the good news.

Act III reveals Mosca and Bonario conversing in the street. For some reason, Mosca is telling Bonario of Corbaccio's intention to disinherit him and inviting the son to witness the deed at Volpone's house. Meanwhile, Lady Would-be visits Volpone and nearly talks him to death. Mosca gets rid of her by saying that Sir Politic was lately seen rowing in a gondola with a cunning courtesan. Corvino arrives, dragging his unwilling wife into the fox's lair; Volpone, left alone with the shrinking lady, is not successful in his persuasive attempts to seduce her. Just as he is about to take her by force, Bonario leaps from his hiding place and denounces Volpone and spirits the lady to safety.

Mosca saves Volpone from the police by explaining the incident to the three gulls and persuading them to tell his contrived story in court. Mosca says that Bonario, impatient to see Volpone, discovered the fox with Celia, seized the lady, and made her swear that Volpone had attempted to rape her. The plan is to get an injunction against Bonario.

Act IV begins with the subplot of Sir Politic Would-be and Peregrine. Sir Politic is discovered entertaining his fellow Englishman with his naive understanding of politics. Lady Would-be interrupts the conversation and mistakes Peregrine for the courtesan. She apologizes upon discovering her mistake, but Peregrine leaves in a huff and promises to take his revenge for the affront.

At the court, Voltore succeeds in making Celia and Bonario look like lovers. Mosca persuades Lady Would-be to testify that Celia was the bawd in the gondola with her husband. Volpone makes his entrance on a stretcher to demonstrate his impotence.

All augurs well for the rogues as the fifth act begins. But Volpone cannot leave well enough alone. He sends his servants to announce his demise and waits for the gulls to come to claim their inheritance. Mosca is the heir! The parasite flaunts his knowledge of their wrongdoing to the birds of prey and they leave in despair. Disguised as a police officer, Volpone follows them to taunt them further.

Meanwhile, Peregrine, disguised as a merchant, comes to Sir Politic's house and tells the knight that the police are seeking him because he has plotted to overthrow the Venetian state. When Sir Politic hides in a tortoise shell, Peregrine calls in some other merchants to mock and humiliate the foolish Englishman.

At the court, the three gulls, enraged by Mosca and Volpone and the loss of their hopes, decide to tell the truth. They accuse Mosca of being the lying villain who created the whole plot. Mosca is summoned and arrives with another plot in mind. He will extricate Volpone from this predicament, but the fox must remain dead and he, Mosca, must continue as the heir. Volpone throws off his disguise and the entire intrigue is revealed.

The court sentences Mosca to the galleys; Volpone is deprived of his goods and sent to a hospital for incurables. The gulls are deprived of a legal practice, a wife, and a fortune. Celia returns to her father with her dowry trebled, and Bonario is his father's heir immediately.

LIST OF CHARACTERS

Volpone

A rich Venetian nobleman who compounds his wealth by feigning fatal illness while promising several greedy friends he will make them his heir.

Mosca

A parasite, Mosca is a fellow of no birth, without hope of worldly advancement beyond sharing the ill-gotten gains of his master. He is Volpone's chief minister and plot-maker.

Voltore

This vulture is an advocate who can speak well in any cause. He aids Mosca to fleece others, thinking that the wealth will eventually come to him.

Corbaccio

An extremely old gentleman, Corbaccio expects to dance on Volpone's grave. He disinherits his son to make his position as Volpone's heir secure.

Corvino

A typical jealous husband who is persuaded by his greed to look like a cuckold.

Celia

Corvino's beauteous wife is as pure as the driven snow.

Bonario

A young gentleman of Venice, son to Corbaccio, and an honest man.

Sir Politic Would-be

An English knight whose mind and notebooks are filled with naive intrigues and playbook political plots.

Lady Would-be

Sir Politic's loquacious and homely wife, who attempts to join the greedy gulls in fleecing Volpone.

Peregrine

An English tourist in Venice.

Nano

Volpone's dwarf.

Androgyno

A hermaphrodite and professional fool employed in Volpone's household.

Castrone

Volpone's servant, a eunuch.

Four Avocatori, a Notario, Officers of the Court, and three Mercatori

These extras round out the persons needed to conduct the business of the court and expose the plotters.

SUMMARIES AND COMMENTARIES

ACT I – SCENE 1

Summary

Volpone, a gentleman of Venice, is discovered at home rhapsodizing about his wealth, that "sacred treasure in this blessed room." His servant Mosca impishly sings the harmony to his master's praise of gold. Volpone treasures the manner in which the gold comes to him.

Heirless Volpone attracts the greedy and wealthy to his house; they bring with them plate, coin, and jewels in the hope that his imminent death will return their gifts tenfold. The gift-giving competition is whetted by Volpone's clever feigning of serious illness. While savoring the success of his ruse, Volpone summons his eunuch, dwarf, and fool to celebrate his present triumph with an interlude, a brief, comic, playlike sequence.

Commentary

The play is set in Renaissance Italy; the characters take their names from animals and birds. The plot grew out of a beast fable popular in the Elizabethan oral tradition. *Volpone (volpe)* means fox in Italian; *Mosca* is the word for parasitic gadfly. Mosca is dependent upon the goodwill of the sly Volpone. Volpone's genius lies in his ability to fleece the greedy rich, the covetous wealthy, without resort to trade, venture, or product, the usual methods of commercial advancement. Furthermore, no poor, ignorant person is harmed, and several parasites are maintained in husbanding the gold.

Two types of parasites or fools are found in the courts of Renaissance gentlemen: the natural idiots or deformed fools (for example, the dwarf, eunuch, and fool who entertain Volpone) and the obsequious but clever fools (for example, Mosca). The others are fools by nature; Mosca plays the fool by choice.

It is important to note that although Volpone is a gentleman and not a parasite, he is nonetheless making his living by employing the methods of such fools. Despite his noble heritage, Volpone chooses the occupation of a parasitic fool. This indicates that he is to be a comic and not a serious figure.

The locale of Scene 2 is the same as that of Scene 1. Each scene begins on the entrance of a new character. These are often called "French scenes," and their unity rests in the revelation of the quality of a new character, the demonstration of his chief characteristics by example, and the contribution he will subsequently make to the play's conflict.

ACT I – SCENE 2

Summary

The scene begins with the interlude performed by the deformed fools of Volpone's household. At its conclusion, the first dupe arrives outside Volpone's residence. Voltore (the vulture) is an advocate by profession and a gull by avocation. Volpone hurries to change into his costume of a decaying carcass. He dons a long gown, covers his head with a nightcap, and climbs under the fur coverlets of his supposed deathbed. All is in readiness for Mosca to bring in the victim. Mosca appears with Voltore's rich gift of an exquisitely carved gold plate engraved with the arms and name of Volpone. Mosca, hardly able to contain his glee, tells Volpone of the greedy anticipation of Voltore.

Commentary

The interlude performed by the eunuch, dwarf, and fool is a satire on the kind of comic relief injected between the acts of a morality play. Jonson's dialogue imitates the false pace of such verse while demonstrating his command of the literature of the ancients. The playwright takes the opportunity to show his contempt for the policies of Puritanism by arguing for the Pythagorean rule over that of reformed religion. In the end, the fools of the interlude suggest that it is best to suffer neither rule; as

Mosca's song indicates, the fool's condition is best:

> Fools they are the only nation
> Worth men's envy or admiration,
> . . . .
> E'en his face begetteth laughter,
> And he speaks truth free from slaughter.

The fool lives outside the social order and can speak the truth because he is not responsible for what he says. Mosca has chosen this course for himself.

Ben Jonson was a man of some classical learning as well as an accomplished man of the theater. His satire of the poorer professional players of the traveling morality drama gives him a chance to demonstrate his theatrical superiority. His larding of the dialogue of this interlude with Greek names serves to show his familiarity with the classics.

In the tradition of the beast fable, the name *Voltore* characterizes the gull as a bird of prey. The vulture hovers outside the rooms of the fox waiting for his victim to die.

The playwright has established the atmosphere of the proceedings. He has introduced the audience to his two leading characters and set up the circumstances of their mischievous ruse. At the same time, he has mocked players, Puritans, and the foolishness of the world which comes to Volpone's very house to be gulled.

The reader should note Jonson's understanding of theatrical technique. The playwright has afforded his leading actors a chance to employ what performances call "sight gags" (visual humor); for example, Volpone dresses in an elaborate invalid's costume in preparation for Voltore's entrance. Throughout the play, Jonson has prepared places in the action for just such byplay. The beastiary character names are also visually suggestive. An authority on Ben Jonson's plays, Robert E. Knoll, believes that "if we fail to visualize the scenes and the movements on stage, we miss half the fun and two-thirds of Jonson's dramatic genius."

ACT I – SCENE 3

Summary

Mosca tells Voltore that Volpone holds the vulture first in his love. The present is offered Volpone; the value of the gift evokes Volpone's suggestion that Voltore come more often. Voltore feigns sadness at the pitiful sight of Volpone. Mosca shares the private asides of both Volpone and Voltore as he moves across the stage between them. He encourages both actors to exaggerate their false conditions. Mosca assures the advocate that all of Volpone's wealth will soon pass into the lawyer's coffers. The drooling gull is interrupted by the knocking of another aspirant to Volpone's hoard, one Signior Corbaccio (carrion crow). Mosca hurries the fleeced Voltore out, promising him a copy of Volpone's will. The two conspirators, Volpone and Mosca, rejoice at the first victim's folly and prepare for the entrance of the next fool.

Commentary

Voltore's entrance presents the audience with its first opportunity to watch the central action of the play. It is evident that all of the actors are playing their own game. Volpone must feign deathly illness and rely upon Mosca as his interpreter and cohort. Voltore, too, relies on Mosca to secure the will in his favor. The parasite Mosca depends upon Volpone's munificence, which is directly related to the success of their ruse.

While the gadfly Mosca goes from the fox to Voltore and back to the fox, the vulture hovers near his dying prey and Volpone plays dead to trick the hunter. The names of the characters indicate not only their emotional dispositions, but even the affected way in which they move during the action of the play.

Jonson has intended some comment upon the fact that the vulture is a lawyer. Mosca wisely appeals to Voltore's greed by referring to his weakness for things in writing, specifically, Volpone's will. It is a fine comic insight into human character.

Voltore's scene is ended by the announcement of the entrance of another gull. The playwright allows Voltore to learn of his competition for Volpone's gold. He is building the audience's comic expectation. (The audience is aware of the entire ruse.) The reader should keep these mounting complications in mind because they represent the gradual progression of the comic mood.

ACT I – SCENE 4

Summary

Though Corbaccio is older and more impotent than Volpone could ever pretend to be, he hopes to hop over Volpone's grave. The carrion crow has purchased a drug for Volpone, which Mosca wisely refuses on his master's behalf. Mosca mocks the medical profession, saying that when a doctor kills a man, the law not only absolves him but gives him great rewards. Mosca relates Volpone's worsening condition by illustrating the approach of death on the face of Corbaccio. Corbaccio is pleased that Volpone is near death. Mosca cleverly obtains Corbaccio's gift of a bag of gold sequins by reminding him that Voltore left the gold plate.

Not to be satisfied with a mere bag of gold, Mosca, with cozening audacity, persuades the old, decaying Corbaccio to disinherit his brave, noble son in favor of Volpone. Corbaccio will surely outlive Volpone and the fox will gratefully, after so great a display of affection by Corbaccio, make the old crow his heir. Eventually, the son will get all of Corbaccio's inheritance and more.

Corbaccio's distracted delight, coupled with his bad hearing, enables the bold Mosca to tell him to his face that his knowledge is no better than his hearing. Volpone, playing the bedridden sick man, can hardly cover his laughter as Corbaccio exits. The two rogues re-create their triumph with gales of laughter until they are interrupted by the knock of Corvino (the raven).

Commentary

Corbaccio, as the name suggests, is an old crow ready to die, living only on carrion. He is not as fearsome a bird of prey as the vulture, and Mosca is bolder in his presence. This boldness is evident in two excellent pieces of visual "business." In mimic fashion, Mosca illustrates Volpone's death throes on Corbaccio's face. Again, Mosca employs Corbaccio's hearing defect to mock his infirmity. The actor's facial expression and vocal tone belie the meaning of his rhetoric.

Hyperbole is the rhetorical device of exaggeration for effect, and not to be taken as literal speech. Usually, hyperbole is used as an ornament to speech. In Jonson's case, it is an essential part of the dramatic fun. Mosca's use of hyperbole has special ironic power. He is exaggerating Volpone's condition but not Corbaccio's present state of health. Jonson's use of hyperbole as a rhetorical device in *Volpone* enriches the meaning of the dramatic situation. The hyberbolic intensity of the play's rhetoric increases as the plot complications become more involved.

Mosca's attempt to get Corbaccio's will made out to Volpone increases the plot complications. It is not to be supposed that the old crow's son will take his disinheritance lying down. Mosca has created another complication by cheating an innocent person.

ACT I – SCENE 5

Summary

Mosca tells Corvino that Volpone does not even recognize old friends in his present condition. On cue, the delirious Volpone weakly drawls "Signior Corvino." Mosca announces that his master's hearing is gone, but he can feel the gem Corvino has brought. Corvino feigns sorrow over Volpone's condition, but

Mosca discourages this act. After all, what difference does it make now that Volpone cannot hear them. Mosca uses this ruse to attack his employer, declaring that Volpone has only bastard children begot on beggars, Gypsies, Jews, and Blackmoors. Volpone is powerless to reprimand his parasite because he must continue to feign deafness. Mosca heaps on the insults, saying that the dwarf, fool, and eunuch are Volpone's natural children! Encouraged to join the game, Corvino pledges Mosca a share of his inheritance in exchange for the gadfly's assistance. Mosca suggests that part of Corvino's fortune is his gallant wife! This causes Corvino to make a quick exit. Another knock indicates the presence of Lady Would-be, the wife of the English knight Sir Politic Would-be.

Volpone tells Mosca to get rid of her, wondering that the "bold English...dare let loose their wives to all encounters!" Mosca says that with her face she cannot help but be honest (virtuous). Mosca makes a hymn to the beauty of Corvino's wife, and Volpone resolves to see the lady. A disguise must be designed to deceive the insanely jealous Corvino; he guards his wife with ten spies!

Commentary

Corvino is a preening raven; his greatest treasure is his beautiful wife. Mosca sees this character flaw and plays upon it by suggesting that she might be shared with the rest of his fortune. It is a telling remark. It also serves to warn of a future plot development. Corvino's wife will surely be a pawn in the villainous game. Jonson is preparing us for her entrance.

The playwright employs the actors' skills in the suppressed anger and frustration of Volpone, the impish delight of Mosca, and the foolish recklessness of Corvino as each deceives the other. The use of hyperbole is especially ironic and effective in revealing Mosca's character. He is the servant of all, but he has no affection or loyalty for anyone. It is a business deal, and, if he can cover his fun, the gadfly is glad to sting anyone. Furthermore, Corvino's use of abuse is particularly ironic because he is unaware of its real effect. He is being the subtle fool! Notice that only the audience is aware of these complications. Volpone is angry at the insults and frustrated that he cannot reply, but he does not suspect that this is the first indication of the treatment to which he subjected himself when he decided to play the fool. He has the fool's license; he also has the fool's lowly social position. Corvino is preoccupied with his own folly, and Mosca is impressed by the power of his own audacious behavior.

Though the play is set in Italy, Jonson has already satirized London Puritanism. In the last sequence, he prepares us for the English tourist Sir Politic Would-be. Sir Pol suggests the poll parrot, and the English fools are bumbling and ineffectual mimics of the fools of the main plot. Lady Pol is a burlesque of the three birds of prey.

The three gulls have been robbed of their gold, and Mosca promises to relieve them of larger treasure. The gold belongs to whoever can take it. So Volpone and Mosca become involved in stealing innocent beauty.

Until this moment, the action has taken place in Volpone's palace. The world has come to him to be fleeced. Now the fox must leave the safety of his lair and risk capture.

ACT II – SCENE 1

Summary

Jonson begins the second act by introducing his audience to a couple of English tourists sightseeing in St. Mark's Square. Sir Politic Would-be is in Venice at his wife's insistence; it is the height of the social season. Peregrine is confused by Sir Pol's strange conversation: "This fellow, does he gull me, trow, or is gulled?" Sir Pol mysteriously asks of signs and portents current in London. Affecting the same disposition, Peregrine relates the death of the fool Stone. "Stone dead!" puns Sir Pol in unconscious shock, and Peregrine hopes that the fool "was no kinsman" to the knight. Sir Pol tells Peregrine that Stone was actually a dangerous secret agent who "received weekly intelligence" in a "trencher of meat" and "before the meal was done, convey[ed] an answer in a toothpick." Peregrine repeats that he has heard "your baboons were spies" and Sir Pol gravely concurs. Anxious to mark the ebbs and flows of states, Sir Politic keeps a notebook filled with pertinent observations. At that moment, Mosca and the dwarf enter the square and begin erecting a stage. They are disguised.

Commentary

The first act of *Volpone* develops the central conflict and introduces the main characters of the play. Jonson begins the second act with the people and action of the parallel subplot. The most obvious parallel is the gullible nature of Sir Politic, whom Peregrine uses as his fool.

Jonson uses Sir Pol's political machinations as a prologue to the more serious schemes connected with Volpone's mountebank disguise. Furthermore, Sir Pol represents the credulous audience before whom Volpone is about to play.

Peregrine is a pilgrim falcon. The falcon, a bird of sport, is commonly trained to hunt other birds. The subplot characters imitate the actors of the main plot, but that is their major folly. The game they play is not a serious one, and the outcome is not as harsh as the conclusion of the main plot.

ACT II – SCENE 2

Summary

Mosca has the stage placed beneath the windows of Corvino's house in St. Mark's Square. Peregrine describes mountebanks as "quacksalvers, fellows that live by vending oils and drugs." Sir Pol protests that such mountebanks are "great general scholars" and "excellent physicians." Sir Politic asks the disguised Mosca for the name of the mountebank about to take the stage. Mosca names an Italian juggler who was in England about that time, Scoto of Mantua. At that moment, Volpone enters, as Scoto, followed by a crowd.

Volpone attacks the methods of other mountebanks, those "turdy-facy-nasty-paty-lousy-fartical rogues." Scoto, alias Volpone, declares that, unlike other mountebanks, he has nothing to sell. Sir Pol smiles smugly at Peregrine. At once, Volpone draws forth a "precious liquor," crying "O health! Health! The blessing of the rich! The riches of the poor!" Peregrine smiles knowingly, but Sir Pol is completely fooled. Volpone wants eight crowns for this elixir, which can cure *vertigine, mal caduco, tremor cordia*—in short, everything from dandruff to athlete's foot. A song is extemporized, a seventeenth-century singing commercial, and Volpone launches into the final pitch.

He promises to give away his expensive elixir to anyone who will give him a memento, a handkerchief. He looks to the balcony of Corvino's house, where Celia has been listening intently. Suddenly, she throws down her handkerchief. Volpone speaks directly to her and, with great desire in his voice and words, promises to give her a powder more potent even than the oil of Scoto.

Commentary

Act II is composed of two actions. The first is the preparation for, and the appearance of, the mountebank, Volpone. This includes the action of the subplot between Sir Politic and Peregrine and the performance of Volpone as Scoto of Mantua, whose real name was Dionisio. The derivation from Dionysus, Greek god of wine, brings to mind the pagan festival of fertility, a time of wild debauchery and hilarity. The figure of the god Dionysus had a reputation for changing its shape. The special irony of Volpone's disguise is that it describes the proceedings as a pagan festival, with Volpone as the god of wild license and many faces. Elizabethans were familiar with holidays of this kind, and they called the central actors of such festivals "mummers." At the end of each festival, it was customary that the god or prince of the debauchery be burned in effigy, to the great delight of the participants. Jonson's audience expected Volpone to be sacrificed at the end of the fun.

The first four scenes of Act II take place on St. Mark's Square before Corvino's house. Like those of the first act, they begin with the entrance of a new character. The locale prevails until the first action is completed.

The dialogue is in blank verse except during the mountebank's pitch. Volpone's sales talk is purposeful and pragmatic. It is important to remember the presence of Mosca during Volpone's oratory. Though he hasn't a line, he engineered the performance and knows which is Celia's window. He is the device that focuses Volpone's and our attention on her presence in the window.

Jonson's rhetoric for Scoto has all of the enchantment associated with carnival barkers. The irony of the exaggerated language is in the dramatic situation. The language demands that the actor playing Scoto be able to perform well in the role of a mountebank. Volpone is more than competent; he is cast to type. Mosca is clever enough to draw our attention to this irony.

Finally, it is evident that the fox is out of his lair. Volpone's action was previously confined to his feigning illness from his "deathbed." Now he seizes control of the play's action. Out of his usual domicile, the fox puts on a disguise.

ACT II – SCENE 3

Summary

Corvino suddenly rushes from his house, screaming at and beating on the disguised Volpone, demanding that he leave instantly. Does Scoto of Mantua intend to make Corvino a Pantalone and his wife a Franciscina? Sir Politic interprets this unexpected excitement as a trick of state and beats a hasty retreat. "This knight," says Peregrine, "I may not lose him, for my mirth, till night."

Commentary

The central figure of much festival comedy was the cuckold. The word is said to be an allusion to the cuckoo bird's habit of laying its eggs in the nests of other birds. Corvino, a proud and preening raven, is about to be turned into a cuckoo bird! Aware of this threat to his reputation, he refers to the *commedia dell'arte* characters of the cuckold and his wife, Pantalone and Franciscina. A traveling *commedia dell'arte* troupe had recently played in London, and Jonson alludes to these comedians as a parallel to the action of his play. It was traditional with mountebanks to beat them for their labors. Harlequin of the *commedia* was the fool who tried to trick Pantalone and was beaten for his trouble. Harlequin was a base fellow and generally deserved the blows. Volpone, disguised as Scoto, is beaten by Corvino as a base mountebank about to cuckold him. It is ironic that, once again, the fox cannot reveal his true identity without risking disaster. The human Volpone is beginning to lose his identity. The animal Volpone is a perversion of humanity. The special dramatic significance of the animal names is becoming more apparent.

ACT II – SCENE 4

Summary

After the crowd disperses in confusion, Volpone and Mosca stagger down to the front of the stage in great distress. Volpone has been wounded by "angry Cupid, bolting from her [Celia's] eyes." Volpone must see her or die a wretched man. Though the meeting seems impossible, Mosca undertakes to turn the trick. Volpone offers Mosca everything for a meeting with Celia. Mosca consoles Volpone's longing by promising him success in cuckolding Corvino. Volpone is pleased that he played the mountebank so successfully. Mosca tells his master that "Scoto himself could hardly have distinguished!"

Commentary

Now that Volpone has discovered for himself the beauty of Celia, she becomes another desired possession. The important thing is that she already belongs to Corvino. Volpone's greed is reserved for objects that others possess. Mosca is fully aware of this character trait, and he teases Volpone's longing with the promise of making Corvino a cuckold. Celia is not desired because of her beauty; rather, her beauty makes tricking Corvino worth the effort. Volpone's greed has completely mastered him.

The servant Mosca is aware that Volpone is now a slave to his own greed. Volpone even desires the parasite to praise his performance as a fool! When Mosca responds with lavish praise, Volpone is too preoccupied with his desires to hear the irony in his servant's voice.

Jonson ends the scene without disclosing how he means to have Mosca bring about the meeting between Volpone and Celia. This mystery adds comic anticipation to the suspense of the plot.

ACT II – SCENE 5

Summary

The action shifts to a room in Corvino's house. The raven is furious with Celia for flirting with the disguised Volpone. Celia has rendered death to his honor by making eyes at the city's fool. Perhaps she would like to play Lady Vanity of the morality plays to mortify him further.

Innocent Celia pleads for her lord's patience. It is of no avail; Corvino threatens her with death. She cannot understand the gravity of the situation, and this intensifies Corvino's rage. Corvino suggests that the innocent handkerchief possessed a message of assignation. Celia is horrified at the thought, and Corvino declares his intention of compounding his precious restrictions upon her. "I will keep thee backwards; thy lodging shall be backwards, thy walks backwards." This is his reward for being open with her, allowing her to go to church every once in a while; he has been taken advantage of. Suddenly, a knock stops up his rage, and he hustles Celia out of the room with harsh threats. A servant announces the presence of Signior Mosca.

Commentary

Corvino is the prototype of the jealous husband. Corvino is an Italian, not a Dutchman! Flirting with his wife is the worst insult that can be paid an Italian gentleman. Jealousy is Corvino's ruling passion. Jonson is preparing us for a development of the plot.

If Corvino is insanely jealous, Celia is incredibly virtuous. She is prim, humorless, and without any understanding of her husband. She is a dramatic cliché; she is the heroine caught in the clutches of a foul ravisher. She is the prototype of the sweet, innocent, pure-as-the-driven-snow heroine. Jonson does not ask his audience to pity her; he wants us to laugh at her.

Once again, Jonson refers to the theater of his time. Lady Vanity of the morality drama was played as a courtesan, but she was also a figure of fun. Jonson wanted the comic parallel to his character made clear. Celia is vain about her innocence, and Corvino thinks she is impure.

This scene is a very important plot sequence. It introduces us to the character of Celia, prepares for Corvino's betrayal of an Italian's honor, and sets the scene for Volpone's greatest trick. The reader must remember that the action started in the fox's lair, moved into the open of the streets of Venice, and is now located in the bird's nest.

ACT II – SCENE 6

Summary

Corvino turns from wrath to wreathed smiles in anticipation of the announcement of Volpone's death. Alas, Mosca dashes his hopes with the news that Scoto's oil has effected Volpone's recovery. Furthermore, the blessed juice was procured for Volpone by Corbaccio and Voltore. They have hired a physician to prescribe "a flayed ape clapped to his breast," and "some young woman must be straight sought out, lusty, and full of juice, to sleep by him." Corvino perceives Voltore's and Corbaccio's threat to his hopes and suggests that Mosca hire a courtesan on his behalf. Mosca rejects this course of action as too dangerous. They "may perchance light on a quean [who] may cheat us all."

Mosca describes the simple creature they must find, using Celia as the model of his inspiration. In mock despair, Mosca asks Corvino: "Ha' you no kinswoman?" One of the doctors offered his own daughter! Corvino is shocked. Mosca assures him that the doctor did so knowing that "naught can warm his [Volpone's] blood." Corvino grasps Mosca's intention and mulls over the possibility of Celia's becoming his candidate. Suddenly, the doctor is a covetous wretch and Corvino's honor is forgotten. Mosca feigns surprise and compliments Corvino on his audacious plan. Corvino's zeal hurries Mosca to make the proper preparations. Mosca promises that only Corvino will be received. There is only one condition Corvino must accept: he must not come until he receives word from Mosca.

Commentary

Mosca is now at the top of his cozening form. Not only does he grant Volpone a miraculous recovery, but he attributes it to the imposter's own oil! The delight of the following rhetoric is based upon the audience's understanding of Mosca's aim and their interest in watching him construct his plot. The ironic power of the description of Celia is the result of the audience's awareness of Mosca's audacity.

The second action of Act II establishes Corvino's insane jealousy and Mosca's appeal to the stronger of his passions, greed. Mosca demonstrates great understanding of Corvino's nature in his subtle phrasing of the appeal.

It is especially ironic to observe that Jonson has allowed Corvino to be cuckolded in his own house!

It is also important to note Corvino's excessive, lengthy, and jealous tirade on fidelity, his quick reversal of form, and, finally, his warm sympathy for his wife. These emotional transitions demand a sophisticated comic touch and a delicate sense of timing, attributes found only in great character actors.

In the last analysis, it is not Mosca's audacity, or Volpone's cunning performance, that cuckolds Corvino. It is his own comic flaw that exposes him to this final humiliation. The flaw is greed. All of the characters in *Volpone* are brought down by this trait.

ACT II – SCENE 7

Summary

Corvino summons his wife, who enters blubbering. The raven disclaims all jealousy and commands Celia to dress in her best attire; they are going to a feast at Volpone's house. There, predicts Corvino, "it shall appear how far I am free from jealousy or fear."

Commentary

Corvino persuades his wife that he is not the typical Italian gentleman. He is not jealous, and he will cuckold himself to prove it! It is a delicious piece, and, best of all, the ironic gull is unaware of the irony!

The second action of Act II is complete. The suspense begins to mount as the complications follow quickly, one upon the other. The audience is aware that Mosca is now in control of Volpone's fate. In such a position of power and with the possibility of sharing his master's gold, will the servant be satisfied with the leavings from Volpone's table? Remember, Mosca is a parasite, a servant, a man without hope of advancement. His only delight is to mock his social superiors. He has not displayed any greedy tendencies because there was no hope of fulfilling his desires. Celia may yet prove to be the foil by which Mosca can attain mastery of his master.

ACT III – SCENE 1

Summary

Mosca is discovered in the street, soliloquizing on the nature, number, and the kinds of parasitic fools.

Commentary

Once again, the act is divided into two locales. The first two scenes take place on a street. It is necessary that we become more completely acquainted with Mosca's disposition. Thus the third act opens with the traditional Elizabethan theatrical convention of the soliloquy.

In Mosca's address to the audience, Jonson displays a sound acquaintance with the history of the fool. There are parasites who subject themselves basely "to please the belly and the groin." There are others who fawn and make their voices as echoes to their lords. "But your fine, elegant rascal, that can rise and stoop, almost together, like an arrow," this "creature had the art born with him"; his kind are "the true parasites, others but their zanies." Furthermore, Mosca does not consider that his profession is an inferior one. Rather, "almost all the wise world is little else, in nature, but parasites or sub-parasites." Mosca is the equal of Volpone, Voltore, Corbaccio, and Corvino. It is not that he is able to rise to their noble position; they have made him their equal by descending to his lowly state. Jonson offers the audience a key to the comic philosophy of the play. The Elizabethan was acquainted with the profession of folly. There were two kinds of fools: the mentally and physically deformed fools of nature (for example, the dwarf, eunuch, and fool of Volpone's household) and those who play the fool by choice (such as Mosca). These deformed creatures reminded even kings that they were mortal. The nobility possessed certain human qualities in common with fools. If too much emphasis is place on the pleasures of the "belly and the groin," or on flattery and trickery, we ironically diminish our humanity.

The soliloquy is an important theatrical device. It enabled the playwright to comment on the action of the play as well as to reveal the inner thoughts and feelings of the speaker. In this case, Jonson employs it as a quiet interlude before the plot begins to hurdle out of the characters' control to a final comic conclusion. Up to this point, as Mosca's attitude suggests, the villains are the complete masters of events. Things are about to get out of hand.

ACT III – SCENE 2

Summary

Mosca's musings are interrupted by Old Corbaccio's son, Bonario (good fellow). The parasite attempts to speak with the young man, but Bonario is "loath to interchange discourse" with such a person. Unperturbed, Mosca rejects the direct insult of "baseness" and falls into a lament upon the accident of his birth. After a well-modulated refrain of self-pity, Mosca weeps. Bonario is moved by this display of softness and repents his harshness. Seizing this opening, Mosca recites a litany of his villainies perpetrated before the audience's eyes, then denies his association with such corruption. Bonario cannot believe that anyone could dissemble such a passion, and he begs Mosca's forgiveness for so mistaking his nature.

Now the thread of Mosca's purpose becomes apparent. He warns Bonario that his father intends to disinherit him. Bonario begins to suspect Mosca of some trickery. Equal to this turn of events, Mosca praises Bonario for remaining faithful to his filial duty. Such devotion, says the gadfly, only makes the wrong more monstrous. In order to prove himself honest, Mosca offers to bring Bonario to witness the deed. Bonario follows Mosca, whose "heart weeps blood in anguish."

Commentary

The irony of the entire plot and language is intensifying with each scene. Mosca tells Bonario the truth, which only he could know. Then he denies he had a part in the revealed plot. The audience knows the truth of the matter and is able to appreciate the magnitude and excellence of Mosca's lie.

The falsehood is told to the gullible Bonario. Jonson ironically mixes truth into the story that tricks this paragon of virtue. Indeed, Bonario is as phony a hero as Celia is a heroine. Surely the costumers would dress their one-dimensional purity in white. They are without emotional depth and sincerity.

The pace is beginning to quicken; the scenes are short and actors sweep on and off stage, into and out of hiding places, taxing the skill of the actors and the funny bone of the audience.

ACT III – SCENE 3

Summary

Meanwhile, at home in his lavish lair, anxious Volpone passes the hour of waiting by watching a performance of his household fools. After a short interlude, a knock interrupts the playing. Volpone hopes for Mosca's return, but the dwarf tells him it is the English lady. Volpone is to be tormented by Lady Would-be, and Mosca is not present to devise a trick to delay her.

Commentary

Jonson locates this and the next six scenes of Act III in Volpone's house. These constitute one continuous action. Volpone and Mosca are now dedicated to adding Celia to their treasure store.

Volpone is being distracted by his grotesques. This is the lull before the storm. Volpone is anticipating news of Celia. The fools prattle about which of them is the best. The dwarf eats little, takes up the smallest space, and considers himself the most valuable. Their foolish dance parallels the main action of the play. Mosca is also the least in social stature; he, too, feels he is the most valuable. The plot to secure Celia is about to begin. Volpone's and the audience's anticipation mounts until a knock at the door to the fox's chamber is heard. Is it Mosca, or, even better, Celia? The playwright intends to mock us and keep our anticipation high by teasing Volpone with a woman willing to be seduced.

ACT III – SCENE 4

Summary

Lady Would-be makes a fashionable entrance and immediately sends the dwarf Nano to find her dressing woman. Volpone and Nano talk to the audience in asides, commenting on Lady Would-be's plumage and preparations. After extensive emergency repair work has been performed, the dressing woman and dwarf exit and Lady Would-be turns her full and impressive person on Volpone. "The storm," says Volpone, "comes toward me."

Volpone complains to Lady Would-be that he suffers from bad dreams. She seizes the occasion to elaborate upon her own horrors, whereupon Volpone begins actually to tremble and sweat. The remedies come thick, gooey, and fast, compounding Volpone's discomfiture. Next, she launches into a half-learned discourse that is interrupted by Volpone's desperate declaration that, according to Plato, the "highest female grace is silence." Plato cannot silence Lady Would-be. His name brings to mind her classical reading, and Volpone has opened yet another of Pandora's boxes. Lady Would-be is inexorable, and only Mosca's appearance saves Volpone.

Commentary

Lady Pol parrots the plot of *Volpone*. She also dresses up for the role. Her cosmetics and clothes symbolize a painted surface hiding a rotten interior. It is a theatrical visualization of the character of the plot of *Volpone*.

The visual symbol is compounded by the language of the scene. Volpone feigns a bad dream in order to put Lady Would-be off. She takes him at his word and carries his simple fiction to the length of a great history. The end result for Volpone is actual sickness. Volpone began the play as a nobleman playing the fool; his performance eventually replaces reality.

The irony of Lady Pol's dialogue is the same as the irony of the play's plot; that is, Volpone is tortured by words and events that are ridiculous and without meaning, but he is responsible for his own torture. Volpone the artist has tricked his victims and suffers in reality for assuming the role of a debased fool. He suffers precisely because he is so convincing. He plays the fox and is reduced to the role of an animal.

This comic interlude is devoted entirely to the subplot. The audience is holding its breath awaiting the arrival of Mosca and Bonario. Why has Mosca brought Bonario to Volpone's house? Has Mosca thrown caution to the winds? Mosca's entrance not only ends the subplot sequence, but promises to start the suspense of the main plot again.

ACT III – SCENE 5

Summary

In a conspiratorial aside, Volpone entreats Mosca to rid him of "my madam with the everlasting voice!" Always the man of business, the parasite asks the fox if Lady Would-be has given a present to Volpone. "Oh, I do not care!" moans the suffering gentleman. "I'll take her absence upon any price." Lady Would-be scents mischief and interrupts the tricksters with an inconsequential gift, a cap she has made. Without noticing the gift, Mosca draws the English lady into conference. He relates having seen Sir Politic "rowing upon the water in a gondola, with the most cunning courtesan of Venice." "Is't true?" demands the incredulous lady. Follow and see, replies Mosca as he deftly relieves the fleeing Englishwoman of her gift. Wisely, and with some swagger, Mosca, perhaps toying the while with the filched cap, expresses confidence that his lie would be accepted without question: "For lightly, they that use themselves most license are still most jealous." Volpone's gratitude is effusively expressed, but it is squelched by the return of Lady Would-be who demands, "Which way rowed they together?" Mosca, unperturbed, points "toward the Rialto." And away she goes!

Mosca tells Volpone to remain at his couch; Corbaccio and the will are at hand. After they are gone, Mosca has more to reveal.

Commentary

Mosca once again demonstrates his understanding of human nature in his manner of dismissing Lady Would-be. He and his master engage in a bit of private humor when Volpone admits that he will take her absence at any price. Of course, the loss to Volpone is the property of Lady Would-be! Notice that, even though the cap is of little value, Mosca remembers to relieve the lady of her present.

Jonson hastens the speed of the developing action by having Lady Would-be return unexpectedly. Furthermore, this sudden and unlooked-for incident parallels the action of the main plot to come. Lady Would-be is agitated, Volpone nearly loses consciousness, but Mosca remains cool. The audience can expect more of the same as the complications increase. Mosca tells Volpone that Corbaccio is at hand, directing Volpone to bed. Volpone goes behind the curtains of the inner stage. It is important to keep in mind that Volpone is not visible at this point in the ction.

ACT III—SCENE 6

Summary

Mosca enters with Bonario in tow and places him in hiding as a knock is heard at the door. Both young men await the entrance of Corbaccio; Bonario in close hiding and Mosca as the welcoming servant.

Commentary

Timing is the important comic element in this developing plot complexion. As he enters, Bonario must barely miss the retreating Volpone. The plot must always be suspensefully on the verge of collapsing. Furthermore, theatrical surprise depends on not giving the audience a chance to catch up with the swift action. At any rate, the situation is clear. Three characters are awaiting Corbaccio; one behind a bed curtain, another in a closet, and the servant center stage.

ACT III – SCENE 7

Summary

The newcomer is not Corbaccio but Corvino! Celia stands shrinking by his side. Mosca asks why Corvino has come before receiving his message. The raven thought Mosca might forget him! "Did e'er man haste so for his horns?" says Mosca in an aside to the audience.

As Corvino takes Celia upstage to whisper his purpose to her, Mosca deftly spirits Bonario from his hiding place to the apron of the stage. Mosca urgently desires that Bonario retreat to an adjoining gallery, where "there are some books to entertain the time." Mosca is all apologies that Corbaccio has delayed his coming. Bonario, beginning to become suspicious, reluctantly agrees to leave the room. Mosca, satisfied that Bonario is out of the way, opens the drapes on Volpone's bed, revealing the prostrate fox lying in wait for the innocent Celia.

At that moment, Corvino and Celia come back downstage, arguing hotly. Corvino angrily cautions Celia against shifts and tricks that might ruin his chances of getting Volpone's wealth. Celia prefers incarceration to dishonor. Corvino commands the obedience of her marriage vows and relates his great hopes for inheritance. He demands that Celia respect his venture. She cannot respect it above his honor. Corvino defines honor as "a mere term invented to awe fools." He greedily contemplates the rewards that await the success of his plans. Celia valiantly declares that her husband's tactic is a sin. Corvino admits the offer would not have been made to a "hot Tuscan blood" or a "professed critic in lechery." But this is different; it is a "pious work, mere charity, for physic, and honest policy to assure mine own." Celia is about to suffer despair.

From his bed, in a delighted aside to Mosca, Volpone exults over his brightening prospects. The fox orders the lamb brought forth to the slaughter. Mosca makes the introduction of Corvino and Celia in the most cuckolding terms, and the greedy raven is grateful for such preference. In fact, as Mosca praises Celia's beauty, Corvino listens with the critical appreciation of a drama critic. Volpone says it is too kind, but it is, alas, too late. Nonetheless, Volpone generously gives Mosca leave to tell Corvino what he has done for him. Celia draws away, requesting death, but Corvino drags her forward, determined to cuckold himself. He furiously threatens her existence; she only declares herself his martyr. He tries to tempt her with his own vice of greed; she remains impervious to his entreaties. Mosca tries to reconcile the two, but Corvino's anger is monumental. "'Sdeath!" he shouts, "If she would but speak to him, and save my reputation."

Mosca persuades Corvino to leave his wife alone with Volpone. Corvino believes modesty prevents Celia from complying with his wishes in his presence. Celia is left alone to lament being "placed beneath the basest circumstance, and modesty an exile made for money."

Suddenly, the fox leaps from his feigned sickbed and begins the chase. Stealthily, Volpone tries to persuade his prey to stand still and be lovingly devoured. Corvino is a rascal, says Volpone, and "sold his part of paradise for ready money." Remember the mountebank at the window? There is nothing Volpone would not do for her love.

Next, the aging lecher tries to seduce the lady with song. Celia remains adamant. In rich and sensuous verse, Volpone recounts the largess he will give her for her favor.

> ... we will eat such at a meal.
> The heads of parrots, tongues of nightingales,
> The brains of peacocks and of ostriches,
> Shall be our food....

Celia cannot be affected with such delights; her wealth is her innocence. She asks Volpone whether he has a conscience. He replies: "'Tis the beggar's virtue." Indefatigably, Volpone evokes sensual delights in classical references, speaking of Ovid, Jove, and Mars. Celia pleads for herself in a most hauntingly ladylike sweetness: "If you have ears that will be pierced, or eyes that can be opened, a heart [that] may be touched, or any part [of you] that yet sounds man about you," please take anger rather than lust as a manly vice. Torture her, kill her, but leave her honor intact! Old Volpone's eyes and ears cannot comprehend the plea. "Think me cold, frozen, and impotent, and so report me? That I had Nestor's hernia thou wouldst think." Like an old satyr, Volpone demands Celia to "yield, or I'll force thee."

One hand to her milky-white bosom, the other across her forehead, Celia cries, "O! Just God!" Stroking his chin in anticipation and leering with delight, Volpone replies, "In vain."

From out his hiding place, Bonario leaps to the rescue in the nick of time, declaiming: "Forbear, foul ravisher! Libidinous swine!" After a magnificently, preposterously gallant speech, Bonario spirits the lady to safety.

Alone and gnashing his villainous teeth, Volpone cries: "I am unmasked, unspirited, undone, betrayed to beggary, to infamy."

Commentary

This scene is the longest sequence in the act and the climax of the play. From this moment on, the plot runs single-mindedly to an inevitable conclusion. The involvement of the plot develops further, but after Bonario's romantic entrance, the solution of the intrigue is never in doubt. The scene begins on this note of fatality.

For the first time, one of Mosca's stratagems misfires: he has prepared for the expected Corbaccio and finds Corvino instead. Stage business is very important here. Mosca distracts Corvino and Celia long enough to get rid of Bonario. But he is in too much of a hurry and the audience senses that Bonario suspects something. This is important. If the audience anticipates that Bonario will return, it adds suspense to the chase.

Jonson not only carefully contrives the suspense of the action, but piles irony on top of irony to demonstrate the preposterous nature of his characters and their situation. Corvino is so anxious to cuckold himself that he believes his honor requires it. When Mosca talks of Celia's desirable qualities, Corvino is proud of her. A special kind of irony is present when a duped character uses means of persuasion without being aware of the real effect. Why is Corvino unaware of the effect? Because he is blinded by his own greed! This use of rhetorical hyperbole compounds the irony.

Jonson has used hyperbole to enrich the comic situation. He has also employed it to illuminate the character of Celia. This is the first sequence in which she speaks at any length. Her language shows her to be a melodramatic heroine. She is a poor defenseless, virtuous, romantic girl in the clutches of a "libidinous swine." Both Celia and Bonario are caricatures of virtue. They are ridiculous and superficial amalgamations of conventional and sentimental ideas of virtue. Thus Volpone's attempted seduction, though crude and cruel by English theatrical standards, is no serious threat at all. Celia is a poser; she is not in the least believable. Bonario's intervention is not just to save the girl; it gives him a chance to play the romantic hero. It also serves to create the ultimate comic complication.

Remember, this is a comedy and not a melodrama. Jonson is interested in making us laugh at humanity. If we sympathize with Bonario and Celia, it is because they have been interpreted in a way contrary to the entire action of the play. Jonson cracks his wit on the foolishness of greedy people; he also laughs heartily at smug, superficial, and sentimental interpretations of virtue.

When Mosca finally leaves Celia with Volpone, the actual comic chase begins. Celia has resisted her husband's demands that she play up to Volpone. In a magnificent inversion of the social order, Corvino demands that she go to Volpone to save his reputation. Here it may be seen that, in Corvino's greedy state of mind, the reputations of the forsworn are destroyed by the despicable honesty of respectable people. It is a true comic picture of the deformity of human greed. Jonson is following savage irony with cruel irony as the situation races toward a comic conclusion. And the chase begins.

The beast fable is again in evidence. The lamb is left to be devoured by the fox. It is the same in our fairy tale for children, *Little Red Riding Hood*. Just like the wolf in that familiar story, the fox in *Volpone* uses all of his lures to capture the innocence of the little girl. The fox begins with logic, ascends to poetry, and finally depends upon his arms and legs. Remember that the dialogue is punctuated by Volpone's pursuit of retreating Celia. Her melodramatic righteousness is spoken while ducking out of Volpone's reach and running around a table. As the chase reaches the point of exhaustion and possible capture, Bonario appears to save the day. It is a marvelous mock-heroic moment and Jonson is undoubtedly satirizing such plays. Volpone is not physically afraid of Bonario. He is afraid the youth will tell all he knows.

For the first time since the plotting began, Volpone is "unmasked, unspirited, undone, betrayed to beggary, to infamy." Mosca's work is cut out for him. Perhaps he will be able to repair the damage, but the tight chain of his plot has been broken. There are sure to be other weak links that will demand all of the fly's cunning to keep the chain from disintegrating. If the chain breaks, the treasure at the other end will be lost forever.

This hilarious scene demands excellent performing preparations. As the complication evolves, the characters enter and exit unexpectedly, just missing each other, and they arrive at exactly the most inopportune moment. This dovetailing must be perfectly timed and increase in speed and tightness as the scene builds to a conclusion. Remember, the audience is in on everything that Volpone and Mosca are up to, but the gulls are not. Thus the audience anticipates the reaction of both the rogues and the gulls as the complication materializes.

ACT III – SCENE 8

Summary

Feigning a wretched state, Mosca enters and offers to let Volpone cut his throat. Before the distraught Volpone has time to take the fly seriously, Mosca proposes a double suicide. Their lamentations are interrupted by a knock at the door. Mosca feels the branding iron of the felon burning into his forehead. Volpone takes to his bed; for the first time his suffering is not entirely feigned. The door opens on Corbaccio.

Commentary

The playwright gives the tricksters some time to demonstrate the scope of their predicament for the audience. Bonario will let the entire state of Volpone's wealth be shouted about Venice. The gulls will cry "cheat" and demand their money back, and Volpone will be known as a fraud and a villain. Mosca is to blame and he is in danger of being beaten by his master. Only more cleverness can save the rogue. He is given a moment's respite, but, shortly, he will have to face two more formidable opponents.

ACT III – SCENE 9

Summary

Mosca tells Corbaccio that Bonario, accidentally acquainted with his father's purpose, entered the house with drawn sword and tried to kill Volpone. He was also looking for his father with the same intent to kill. "This act," says Corbaccio, "shall disinherit him indeed!" At that moment, Voltore slips onstage, unnoticed by the other characters. Corbaccio hopes that Volpone will soon die; he has a dram to help him along.

Suddenly, Mosca discovers the suspicious Voltore. Voltore calls the parasite a villain for feigning his loyalty to both himself and Corbaccio. What is this device of a will about which they were whispering? Mosca arrogantly tells Voltore the plot is in his behalf. He insists that he invited Bonario to these chambers to hear the disinheritance so that the son would destroy the father. If Bonario killed Corbaccio, the law would take the son into custody and Corbaccio's funds would be put into Volpone's will, made out to Voltore. "My only aim was to dig you a fortune out of these two rotten sepulchers."

Alas, though Voltore is convinced of this part of the plot, he demands an explanation for the presence of Celia. Casually, Mosca mentions a visitation to be explained later. The pressing point is that the impatient Bonario seized the lady, wounded her, and made her swear to affirm that Volpone had raped her. That pretext would accuse Corbaccio, defame Volpone, and ruin Voltore's hopes.

Corbaccio, who has been counting Volpone's treasure, is hustled out the door by Voltore. They must find Corvino to tell him the news. Volpone and Mosca have nothing left to do but pray for the success of their latest dodge.

Commentary

The hurtling pace of the third act is picked up again with Corbaccio's entrance. Here the careless, audacious mind of Mosca, displayed under calmer circumstances at the beginning of the act, shows itself calm in the face of disaster. There is a great deal of opportunity for stage business during this sequence. Perhaps when Mosca discovers Voltore skulking around upstage, it is necessary for him to still a violently trembling leg beneath Volpone's bedcovers. Undoubtedly, the old fox, hiding beneath the sheets, is terror stricken. Not so Mosca.

Let us not forget that Voltore is a great advocate. This special pleading of Mosca's is before a competent judge. Voltore has heard of the will and knows that Mosca must have promised that his patron would reciprocate. In the light of such information, the audience is aware of the grandiose magnificence of Mosca's fabrication. It is a lie in every way worthy of its creator.

Once again, Mosca solves his problems by telling some of the truth to all of the gulls. They learn only what Mosca deems necessary to preserve them in a disposition favorable to his purposes. The audience, of course, is aware of Mosca's duplicity. Their delight is twofold. First, under the circumstances, Mosca is impressive in his agility and ability to keep his stories and listeners straight. Second, Mosca is obviously interested in the meaning of truth and the power of words to deceive as well as communicate. When Mosca is telling his half-truths, his language is always filled with ironic puns intended for the appreciation of his fellow plotter, himself, and his audience.

Jonson is also interested in showing that people often see and hear only that which they wish to see and hear. Mosca is a shrewd judge of this trait in his victims. He knows that he cannot fool Voltore with a simple lie. So he emphasizes those parts of the truth that Voltore's greedy disposition will misinterpret. Today, such perception is called a stereotype. All of Jonson's characters are stereotypes. Thus it is doubly funny that one stereotype, Mosca, can smugly comment on the other stereotypes, Corvino, Corbaccio, Voltore, Bonario, and Celia.

As a member of the audience, have you sympathized with any of these people? If so, have you been taken in by your own stereotype? Is Mosca's own downfall embedded somewhere within his own inability to see that his vision may misjudge an event or a person? Jonson has built future unmaskings into the very character quality of his leading figure.

ACT IV – SCENE 1

Summary

The act begins on a Venetian street with the subplot figures of Sir Politic Would-be and Peregrine. Sir Politic is informing and instructing Peregrine on politic behavior. First, Peregrine must never speak the truth. Furthermore, he must profess no religion, learn to handle silver forks at meals, and know the time to eat melons and figs. Peregrine wonders that these diverse points are all equally matters of state.

Sir Politic boasts that he has been among the Venetians for fourteen months and within the first week of his landing they all thought him native born. He searches daily for one he can trust. If he finds such a creature, he will make him rich. Sir Politic's fertile mind has conceived of some ingenious projects. One of his most impressive ideas concerns the quarantine of ships from the Levant that are suspected of having plague aboard. Instead of lying forty or fifty days at the pesthouse, Sir Politic will save that charge and loss to the merchant.

> First, I bring in your ship 'twixt two brick walls
> — but these the state shall venture. On the one I
> strain me a fair tarpaulin, and in that I stick my
> onions, cut in halves; the other is full of loop-
> holes, out of which I thrust the noses of my bel-
> lows.... Now, sir, your onion, which doth natur-
> ally attract th' infection... will show instantly,
> by his changed color, if there be contagion....

Sir Politic shows Peregrine his personal dairy, wherein it is written when last the Englishman used the privy. These are politic notes, insofar as Sir Politic wrote them.

Commentary

After the headlong pace of Act III's conclusion, Jonson wisely begins Act IV with the subplot. The playwright has reached a comic peak, and he must begin building the plot to its final resolution. Jonson could not hope to keep the audience laughing as it should be at the end of the last act. The audience needs a chance to catch its breath and digest the meaning of the preceding action.

Once again, the first scenes of an act take place in the street, and their unity of action is the subplot of Sir Politic. Sir Pol is mocked in this sequence as the typical English tourist. It would still be a good joke in the England of today. The English never seem to change their native habits when they travel abroad. "Only mad dogs and Englishmen," wrote Noel Coward, "go out in the midday sun."

The fantasy of Sir Politic's thought is exposed in several ways. To begin with, he cannot keep his advice from contradicting his aspirations. He warns Peregrine against telling the truth, and in the next breath he tells his fellow tourist that he is looking for someone he can trust! Next, his idea of scientific method is exposed in the onion plan. Finally, we are shown that he hasn't the slightest notion of what is important or not important by the notes he takes of his daily business. Forks and religion, melon and figs, onions and privy—all are of political moment.

In this scene, Jonson indulges himself in the English penchant for self-mockery. Oscar Wilde, George Bernard Shaw, Noel Coward, and John Osborne have continued that tradition into our time.

ACT IV—SCENE 2

Summary

As Sir Politic and Peregrine earnestly inspect Sir Politic's notes, they walk upstage. At that moment, Lady Would-be enters, complaining of the heat's effect on her complexion. She has been informed by Mosca that her husband is with a courtesan. Therefore, she concludes that Peregrine is a lady in man's apparel.

Sir Politic discovers his wife's presence and gravely introduces Peregrine; the lady interrupts, saying that he only appears to be a youth. When Peregrine fails to understand her talk of one gentlewoman to another, she turns on him. She calls him a prostitute, a female devil in a male exterior. When Sir Politic deserts his beleaguered fellow Englishman, Peregrine angrily mocks Lady Would-be's red nose. Before the expected explosion can occur, Mosca arrives on the scene.

Commentary

The Elizabethan audiences thoroughly enjoyed the convention of sexual disguise, and Jonson's use of that device is an inventive inversion of the usual comic approach. Shakespeare, for example, in his pastoral comedies, frequently dressed his heroine in boy's clothes. When it is remembered that the women's parts in Elizabethan productions were played by young boy apprentices, the reader can see the irony of the device. In *Volpone*, Jonson compounds the irony by having a young boy mistaken for a woman disguised as a young boy. Perhaps the playwright intended some gentle satire of his fellow playwright's frequent reliance on a shopworn stage convention.

It is also ironic that a lady who permits herself so much license should be jealous of her husband. Peregrine is not what he seems to Lady Would-be; indeed, he is an innocent bystander in the whole affair. This is a parallel action to the courtroom sequence that will follow. Celia and Bonario are innocent bystanders, but they, too, will be condemned.

ACT IV – SCENE 3

Summary

Lady Would-be declares her injury to Mosca and calls Peregrine naughty names. Mosca explains her mistake, and the lady easily changes her approach to Peregrine. After a blithe apology, she exits on Mosca's arm, leaving Peregrine bewildered. As he leaves the stage, Peregrine promises to take comic revenge upon Sir Politic.

Commentary

Mosca extricates Lady Would-be from a position in which his lie has placed her. He does so because he needs her service in the courtroom. We can be sure he will not hesitate to lie again to such a gullible listener. In this scene Jonson prepares us for Sir Politic's downfall. Peregrine has been injured and will demand retribution. Though Sir Politic's lies have been ineffective, he must be punished for them. His punishment will be less severe than Volpone's, however, because his guilt is less grievous. At the conclusion of this subplot sequence, Jonson delivers us, with Lady Would-be, to the courthouse steps.

ACT IV – SCENE 4

Summary

The three gulls and Mosca stand before the Venetian officers of justice; their case is about to be tried. The *avocatori* relate the court's shock at the whole monstrous story. Mosca introduces his advocate, Voltore, who takes the place of the enfeebled Volpone. The court is curious about Mosca's position, and Bonario describes him as Volpone's parasite, knave, and pander, concluding his tirade by demanding the fox be summoned at once. Voltore assures the court that the sight of Volpone will move their pities rather than their indignation.

Voltore begins his defense of Volpone by accusing Celia of being a "lewd woman" who has been a "close adulteress" to that "lascivious youth" Bonario. Though Corvino has often caught them in the act, his "timeless bounty" forgave them. To erase the memory of that generosity, the two lovers plotted against Corvino. Meanwhile, Bonario's doting father, disturbed by his son's heartless behavior and grieved that he could not prevent such treachery, at last decided to disinherit him.

The story is too exaggerated for the *avocatori* to credit; Bonario and Celia are known to be virtuous. Voltore declares they are the more dangerous for appearing virtuous. Indicting Bonario and Celia as a parricide and a paramour, Voltore accuses them of having been at Volpone's house in order to seek out and destroy Corbaccio. Celia acted as decoy to the plot, and in the scuffle, aged Volpone, bedridden these three years, was thrown naked upon the floor. The aim of the lovers was to discredit Corbaccio's free choice in Volpone, redeem themselves by laying infamy upon Corvino, to whom, with blushing, they should owe their lives.

Bonario declares that Voltore's soul is in his fee, a statement which shocks the court. Voltore patiently accepts the abuse; could a man who would not spare his parent, spare his accuser? As witness to his tale, Voltore calls Signior Corbaccio to the stand. The old crow calls his own son "an utter stranger to my loins." Bonario cannot resist the authority of his father. He is the perfect son!

Signior Corvino is next to take the stand. He declares his wife a whore and, in an effort to further his greedy cause with Volpone, describes his own cuckolding quite realistically. Mosca assures Corvino there is no shame in what he does. Poor Celia swoons at the testimony of her husband.

Mosca shows the court the wound he received in his scuffle with Bonario. Bonario realizes the cleverness of the plot for the first time.

Commentary

The locale of Act IV switches to the senate chamber. The last three scenes deal with the accusation and vindication of the rogues and gulls and the prosecution of the innocent.

As the action begins, only Mosca, Volpone, and the audience are aware of the whole plot development, but even the audience is shown Mosca's plot only gradually. In this way, they can admire his improvisation and audacity. He has persuaded the three gulls to tell his lie. Mosca is undoubtedly a rogue, but he is a delightfully charming one. Like Falstaff, he must not be taken seriously, but there is much fun to be had with him.

During this sequence, it is important to visualize Mosca's movements. The gadfly darts from one bird of prey to the other, telling each that he alone shall inherit Volpone's wealth. He is not above calling each a fool to the others. Each of the three — Voltore, Corbaccio, and Corvino — plays a precarious part in Mosca's prevarication.

Jonson has stylized the four *avocatori,* who speak in one-line sentences. They remind the reader of the silent-movie Keystone Cops, and their dress should be exaggerated.

As Voltore begins his case, it is evident that he has an excellent insight into the human nature of the court. His patience with innocent Bonario is an artful reversal of character values. In view of it, Voltore's own foolishness is delightfully underlined. He is eloquent in defense of his client. The irony lies in the fact that as his professional skills are most subtle and effective, his personal foolishness is most evident. This is equally true of the other two gulls. Corbaccio is convinced his words are preserving his son's inheritance when they are actually ruining the young man. Corvino saves his reputation by declaring his wife a whore and himself a cuckold! Mosca's plot is an excellent use of the materials chance handed him. Finally, Mosca's dexterity in moving calmly from one gull to the other without mixing up his story is worthy of applause. On the stage, the smoothness of these transitions contributes to the pace of the hilarity. Jonson understood what performers might do for this action.

Bonario remains in character throughout the proceedings. He is an ass, and he is unaware of the plot until it is too late. Always in character, Celia manages a very feminine swoon. Neither of the innocents helps the cause of justice.

The reader should be aware of this scene's excellence as courtroom drama. The members of the audience have not heard Mosca's composition, but they know his desperate position. Will justice triumph? Will the *avocatori* see through Mosca's lie? How will Bonario and Celia escape from their predicament? Perhaps the audience senses that Mosca and Volpone will be unmasked. Certainly the comic tradition of the Elizabethan stage demanded their downfall. Still, the important questions of what will undo them and how it will be accomplished remain to be solved.

ACT IV – SCENE 5

Summary

Mosca's next witness is Lady Would-be, who testifies that Celia was the courtesan with Sir Politic in the gondola. Typically, she apologizes to the *avocatori* for her temper at such great length that they have her ejected.

Next, Bonario and Celia are directed to present their witnesses. Alas, they have only their consciences to support their case. "And heaven," says Celia, "never fails the innocent."

At this point, the invalid Volpone, stretched on a litter, makes his grand entrance. Tearfully, Voltore cries out that "here's the ravisher, the rider on men's wives, the great impostor, the grand voluptuary!" Then, reversing his position, Voltore agrees that his client might be dissembling. Bonario eagerly assents to the lawyer's proposition. Voltore suggests that torturing Volpone would prove his sickness. His sarcasm puts Bonario in an evil position. Voltore eloquently concludes his pleading with the declaration that "damned deeds are done with greatest confidence." The court declares Bonario and Celia guilty; the sentence will be handed down that very night.

Mosca praises Voltore and Corvino for their exemplary courtroom conduct. After all, was it not better for the raven to profess himself a cuckold than to have it proved that he was his wife's pander? Corvino maintains it is Celia's fault because she did not go along with the plot from the beginning. Mosca flies to Corbaccio, telling him that the fox's estate is all but in his possession. All that is left to do is to pay the lawyer. Corbaccio undertakes this expense, lest Mosca overpay Voltore from Volpone's treasury. Mosca assures Voltore that his fortune is made, and then, catching Lady Would-be by the arm, he begins to make her the heir as they leave the courtroom.

Commentary

Lady Would-be's testimony is frosting on the cake for the audacious Mosca. He made up the story of the courtesan and the gondola, and now she has come to court to swear to it! She has been blinded by her greed. First she saw Peregrine as a prostitute; now she claims that she saw Celia with her husband.

Celia and Bonario are foolish enough to think that Venetian courts dispense justice when they merely administer the law. Perhaps Jonson is satirizing the gullibility of those who expect justice at the hands of men. He is certainly mocking the courts as he knew them.

Volpone has waited for the propitious moment to make his entrance. It is a theatrical axiom that the star reserves for himself the most opportune moment to make his big appearance. As it turns out, Mosca has stage-managed this whole scene with the same genius he manifested in inventing the plot. Voltore introduces Volpone with melodramatic tears in his eyes. When he calls the fox an imposter, he is unaware of the complete accuracy of his statement. Only Mosca, Volpone, and the audience can revel in the roguery of the situation. The hyperbole again increases the irony of the action.

During this scene, Jonson has provided ample opportunity for byplay between Volpone and Mosca. When Voltore suggests that they torture Volpone, perhaps Mosca must cover the fox's lively reactions. The court misses this bit of action, but the audience is sure to enjoy it. Voltore's concluding statement that the worst deeds are performed with the greatest confidence is another occasion for stage business. Mosca surely condones this assertion.

At the conclusion of the scene, Mosca presents to the audience the complete inversion of vice and virtue. He convinces each of the gulls that his master's treasury is as good as theirs. Corvino has ruined his wife's reputation and his own, and he blames the predicament on Celia for not agreeing to sleep with Volpone! Corbaccio is even induced, by his greed, to pay for Voltore's services. Voltore has used all of his persuasive powers to tell a lie. As a lawyer, Voltore should be seeking to preserve justice. He is paid for his effort; he will pay for his foolishness. Finally, as they parade out of the court, Mosca brings up the rear with plumed-parrot Lady Would-be on his arm. Can he resist winking at the audience as the lights go out?

ACT V – SCENE 1

Summary

Safe at home, Volpone admits having felt terror in the courtroom. "'Fore God, my left leg 'gan to have the cramp." With a bowl of wine, the fox tries to regain his good humor and his old lust for life. "Any device now, of rare, ingenious knavery" would make him happy. Another bowl of wine to fortify the blood, plus Mosca's entrance to supply the knavery, and Volpone's recovery is under way.

Commentary

Once again Jonson begins to build the action of an act from a quiet moment. The important point in this scene is that if he will only let well enough alone, Volpone is safe. The courts and the gulls have been successfully deluded. Nothing can touch him now. Nonetheless, the audience senses that Volpone's desire to cozen people is insatiable. He is the subject and slave of his own need to play the trickster.

ACT V – SCENE 2

Summary

Volpone confesses to Mosca that cozening the court in such a grand manner was worth "more than if I had enjoyed the wench." Mosca is content to let the whole plot rest. "This is our masterpiece; we cannot think to go beyond this." Volpone's praise of Mosca is unstinting, and the two fall to laughing at their late triumph over the court and the innocents. Volpone imitates Voltore's speech to the court; the language and voice are perfect. Mosca asks Volpone if he did not sweat a little. "In troth," says the fox, "I did a little." Voltore made such a great effort on their behalf that he should be very richly cozened. The two rogues are working up gales of laughter; they have all but lost control of themselves. Finally, Volpone promises to vex all of the gulls from this instant. Clapping his hands, Volpone summons his fools. Would they enjoy some farcical entertainment? Then go out into the streets saying that Volpone is dead! They must do it sadly and "impute it to the grief of this late slander." Mosca shall be his reputed heir. Taking a blank sheet of paper, Volpone fixes his name to his last will and testament.

Volpone develops the new plot in the following manner. Mosca is to put on an expensive gown, take up pen and ink, and begin taking an inventory of Volpone's hoard. If anyone should ask after Volpone's body, the fools are to say it was corrupted. Volpone will "get up behind the curtain, on a stool," and watch the circus unfold. While anticipating the reaction of the gulls to this new cozening, the two rogues begin dressing Mosca and arranging Volpone's hiding place. Suddenly, someone is knocking at the door. It is the vulture. The villains get into character for their charade, with Volpone encouraging Mosca to "torture 'em rarely."

Commentary

As the scene begins, Mosca and Volpone repeat their triumph and its satisfaction. Jonson points out Volpone's principal deformity: it is cozening, not merely wealth and wenching, that he enjoys. Volpone did desire Celia, but he enjoyed cuckolding her husband as much and cozening the court more than he would have enjoyed possessing Celia. This is of primary importance in relation to the play's conclusion.

The two dissemblers slowly build their mirth until, under its heady influence, Volpone is induced to throw caution to the winds. Jonson provides his actors with a chance to mimic other actors and the opportunity to envelop the audience with their infectious laughter. They must be *irresistible* rogues.

Almost spontaneously, Volpone succumbs to his greed for cozening. He improvises his own death to bring out the attending greed of the birds of prey. Then, with inspired irony, he imputes that feigned death to the late slander to his good name made in the courts of Venice. Mosca seems unenthusiastic for the moment. He had used all of his cunning to extricate himself from the last close call. Nonetheless, Volpone's spirits have returned, and his invention with them. The inspiration of Volpone's last will and testament changes the whole complexion of the play. Mosca's eyes must begin to regain their roguish glint; his person must seem more determined than lighthearted about the trickery, for this act puts Volpone within Mosca's power and causes his downfall. It also brings out Mosca's humanity.

Until that moment, Mosca was a parasite and was therefore outside the temptations of normal society. Once he is willed the money, he sees his first chance to come up in the world on his own. For the first time, Mosca performs his tricks, not for their own sake or his master's gain, but for his own material advancement. Until now, Mosca has not been subject to greed, the main vice of the play. Greed has succeeded in making men foolish; it will surely do the same to Mosca. So long as he was without ambition, Mosca was superior to his fellow men. He must know that ambition will make him a fool like the others, but he cannot resist the temptation.

ACT V – SCENE 3

Summary

Voltore is pleased to find Mosca taking inventory, but he is suspicious of the gadfly's new garb. For his part, Mosca completely ignores the vulture and his questions. Old Corbaccio comes on the scene with the same questions Voltore has, and Mosca continues to devote his entire attention to the inventory. Finally, Corvino rushes in to ask Mosca if the hour has come.

Volpone peeps out from behind the curtain to have a better look at his joke and is almost discovered when Lady Would-be appears unexpectedly. Corvino asks the counting Mosca for the will, and without missing an item or a beat, Mosca hands it to him. The others gather around to see their fortunes made; Mosca remains preoccupied with his work. Suddenly, the gulls scream their discovery: "Mosca the heir!" Voltore is stunned, and Corbaccio snatches the will from Corvino, who rushes to Mosca demanding, "Is this in earnest?"

Mosca continues his infuriating count, pausing to say only that he is very busy. "Good faith, it is a fortune thrown upon me ...not my seeking." Finally, Lady Would-be demands a direct answer. Mosca's reply is brutal: "Remember what your ladyship offered me to put you in an heir." Undone, Lady Would-be flees from the scene of her compromise. Volpone is pleased at this beginning.

Corvino is the next gull to press his case. Mosca shows him the valuable gifts that Corvino gave to Volpone and that now belong to the gadfly. Mosca is duly grateful for the raven's generosity. Nonetheless, Corvino's greatest gift, his wife, though not a part of the inheritance, makes him a cuckold. Mosca will not betray him; Corvino leaves in frustrated anger. "Rare, Mosca!" says the hidden Volpone. "How his villainy becomes him!"

Voltore's hopes rise as each of the other gulls leaves with empty hands. Suddenly, Corbaccio shouts, "Mosca the heir?" Volpone collapses with laughter, saying "Oh, his four eyes have found it!" Impotent Corbaccio screams epithets at Mosca; the gadfly replies: "Stop your mouth, or I shall draw the only tooth [that] is left." Mosca accuses Corbaccio of the covetous greed that caused him to disinherit his son. The old crow stumbles blindly from the scene.

"Now, my faithful Mosca," begins the vulture, but Mosca's mood remains constant. Mosca flatters Voltore's talent for pleading in court, and the gadfly trusts that the vulture will prosper, while there are men, and malice, to breed causes. As a matter of fact, Mosca, if the need arises, will hire Voltore's talents at a fee. Mosca applies the finishing touch by thanking Voltore for the gold plate he gave Volpone. Voltore's humiliation is complete.

Volpone comes out of his hiding place and showers praise on his parasite. If only he could disguise himself and follow the gulls, he could further enjoy his triumph. Mosca readily agrees to fit his master in a rare disguise. The disguise is an outfit of a *commandadore,* or police officer. Mosca tells Volpone to look for curses. Volpone replies that "the fox fares ever best when he is curst."

Commentary

Mosca begins this sequence with an air of preoccupation. It is the complete reversal of roles that makes this scene so hilarious. The gadfly has lived on the leavings from Volpone's victims; now it is Mosca's turn to be courted. They have come to Volpone's house to hover over his dead body. They have been fooled; there is no body. Instead, they have a wily heir to cope with.

Mosca is formidable personage to these greedy gulls because he knows the crimes their greed has led them to commit. At first, Mosca toys with them. The stage business is particularly funny during the early part of the scene. Mosca's motion is deliberate and the gulls' movements are agitated. Volpone begins the extensive asides employed by the playwright in Act V. These require good timing and a fine sense of the distinction between talking in character to another character and talking confidentially to an audience. During one of the asides, Volpone is nearly discovered upon the unexpected arrival of Lady Would-be. It is the kind of hairbreadth escape that audiences delight in.

In spite of the continued fun, this is a difficult scene for the actor playing Mosca. He must make the transition from a man of pure license, a prince of folly, to a very greedy fool. Jonson accomplishes the transition in the script by suddenly dispensing with the use of hyperbole. Now everyone says exactly what he means. In the hands of an inexperienced actor, the change to a new game will seem harsh and cruel. There is little gaiety in cruelty. It must be remembered, however, that Mosca merely tells the gulls that they have been foiled by their own foolishness. It is a true comic punishment. The *avocatori* and the Venetian court have failed to perceive the iniquity of these villains. Only a fool can bring them to justice. This savage irony is accompanied by Volpone's delight in Mosca's newfound cruelty.

It is Volpone's need for more and more cozening that puts into Mosca's hands a weapon that will bring the whole business down on their heads. The intrigue of the will causes Mosca and Volpone to fall out. As long as their solidarity is unquestioned, these two rogues must prevail. As soon as Mosca has a legal chance to become Volpone's equal, they become adversaries rather than cohorts. But Volpone is slow to understand the situation, and this is what brings about his destruction. Rare Mosca's becoming villainy is delightful when it is used on the gulls. It is ironic that the price of observing and enjoying that villainy is Volpone's own undoing.

Mosca sends the gulls away by reciting their sins to them. The generous way he assures them that he will not reveal their secret to the courts is infuriating. They cannot prosecute him to get the money they desire. The galling part is that, only yesterday, Mosca was a lowly, fawning servant.

Mosca is still a master of human nature. His ironic promise to employ the lawyer's talents for a fee displays his understanding of Voltore. These insults and dismissals at the hands of a parasite and a servant who is beyond the pale of justice are the real comic punishments the playwright has prepared for his foolish gulls. It cannot be the only punishment, for these birds have caused innocent people to suffer. We must go back to the courtroom because Celia and Bonario are to be sentenced there.

Before we get to the courtroom, Volpone's insatiable desire for trickery must set up his ruin. So it is that Mosca agrees to fit his master with a new disguise. It is again ironic that Volpone should dress up as a policeman. It is this disguise that will lead to his apprehension.

ACT V – SCENE 4

Summary

Peregrine, disguised and accompanied by three merchants, enters Sir Politic's house. His design is merely to frighten, not to harm, Sir Politic. The merchants would rather ship him to Aleppo or some other port. Peregrine instructs them to wait until he gets into an argument with Sir Politic before rushing into the room.

As the merchants leave, Peregrine tells a female servant to announce to the English knight that a merchant, "upon earnest business, desires to speak with him." At first, Sir Politic sends word that grave affairs of state occupy him. Peregrine supposes that he is trying to make sausages without one of the ingredients. Finally, Sir Politic deigns to give the disguised Peregrine an audience.

Sir Politic informs the merchant that he has been busily engaged in writing an apology to his wife; she still believes that Peregrine was a disguised prostitute! Peregrine the merchant has a better theory about Peregrine the pilgrim. That Peregrine was a Venetian spy who reported Sir Politic's plot "to sell the state of Venice to the Turk." Sir Politic becomes distraught. Alas, he has no such plot, only notes drawn from playbooks. Merchant Peregrine volunteers to have Sir Politic smuggled aboard a boat to escape capture. A knock at the door nearly gives the English knight a heart attack! His playacting is causing him serious trouble. Suddenly, he remembers an old invention: he puts a shell over his back and tries to behave like a turtle! Peregrine helps him into this foolish contraption and hurries off to burn Sir Politic's playbook notes.

The three merchants, on cue, burst upon the scene. They ask Peregrine who he is, and he replies: "I'm a merchant, that came here to look upon this tortoise." He points to the trapped Sir Politic and the others take up the joke. Peregrine says it is a fish but that one may strike it and tread upon it. They proceed to prod the foolish knight; Sir Politic gallantly, if uncomfortably, tries to keep up the disguise. Finally, Peregrine and the merchants pull off the shell and mock the gartered knight. Peregrine unmasks and tells Sir Politic that they are now even. The merchants have had their laugh, and Peregrine, apologizing to Sir Politic for the funeral of his papers, departs with his accomplices.

Sir Politic seeks out his lady and is told that she, too, is in need of a physic. He determines to shun this place and clime forever.

Commentary

Once again, Jonson holds his audience in suspense by interrupting the main action of the play in order to resolve the action of the subplot. The subplot action closely parallels the action of the main plot. In fact, it suggests the resolution of the main action.

Unlike the main-plot characters, however, Sir Politic is guilty only of playacting offstage. He is really a very dull fellow, afraid of his own shadow, who dreams of an adventurous life. He is a fool, but a harmless one. His trouble with Peregrine is really brought on by his wife. She subjected Peregrine to a tonguelashing that produced in the English tourist a desire to revenge himself on Sir Politic.

It is interesting to note that Sir Politic sees fit to employ a disguise. As we have seen, Act V is heavily larded with disguises. Jonson is obviously making fun of the English theatrical penchant for disguise. Sir Politic's tortoise shell is a work of genius! Peregrine's burning of the incriminating playbook notes compounds the theatrical irony. It is as if Jonson were saying that these silly devices could be done away with if only all promptbooks could be destroyed.

Ultimately, Sir Politic is trapped in his disguise. Is this intended to suggest that Volpone is trapped by his own disguise? It appears significant that Sir Pol chose the slowest possible animal to imitate, for it makes his escape impossible.

When Peregrine and the three merchants uncase their quarry, they are mimicking the final unmasking of Volpone in the last scene of the play. Since those watching the play fully expect Volpone to be discovered, the present scene merely whets their appetite for the event. And so Sir Politic Would-be is gently, though somewhat rudely purged of his foolish humour.

While maintaining audience suspense about the main plot's resolution, Jonson has neatly tied up the subplot. The audience knows that Sir Politic and his wife will not show up at the courtroom. They have already received their punishment.

ACT V – SCENE 5

Summary

Volpone and Mosca enter, disguised, and each congratulates the other on his appearance. Volpone leaves for a moment to go and see what news can be had from the court. Alone, Mosca reveals himself as follows: "My fox is out of his hole, and ere he shall re-enter, I'll make him languish in his borrowed case." Unless, of course, Volpone will come to terms. Mosca dismisses the fools and servants for the day and resolves to "bury him or gain by him.... To cozen him of all were but a cheat well placed."

Commentary

Mosca's threat to uncase Volpone is an echo of the Sir Politic subplot. He puns on the word *bury*, which signifies the will and Volpone's feigned death as well as the actual cozening Mosca plans for him.

Once again, the playwright uses the soliloquy to display Mosca's character and to forewarn us of the possible outcome of his new disposition.

Mosca is correct in his appraisal of his master. However, it is also a good description of Mosca, for he is about to play tricks for his own personal ambitions.

ACT V — SCENE 6

Summary

Corbaccio and Corvino are discovered in a Venetian street talking about the sentence that the court is about to pronounce upon Bonario and Celia. Each assures the other he will stick to his original story at the final hearing. What else can they do? Corbaccio did disinherit his son, and Corvino, but for an accident of timing, would have been the agent of his own cuckolding.

Volpone approaches the two gentlemen in his *commandadore* costume. He elaborately congratulates them on their recent good news, "the sudden good dropped down upon you ...from old Volpone." Their old indignation returns, and they begin to beat Volpone. Both gulls leave in a huff, but Voltore comes on to take their place.

Commentary

The three short street scenes are a comic repetition of Mosca's mocking of the gulls, but Jonson has a reason for it. He wants the audience to see that even gulls can be insulted too much. The audience thinks the gulls are so frustrated they will eventually explode. If they do, the truth will hurt all of the characters in the central plot.

Once again, as soon as Volpone takes up a disguise, he is beaten. It is the fate of all fools to be beaten. In this case, Volpone is delighted by their anger. It is an excellent indication of the success of his ruse.

ACT V — SCENE 7

Summary

Voltore is grumbling about Mosca's knavery. Volpone tells him that the court awaits his coming, and the fox begins to supplicate for some of the rents from a tenement house owned by the deceased Volpone. When the meaning of the request dawns on Voltore, he vents his spleen on the head of Volpone. With a parting insult, Volpone runs for the next corner.

Commentary

These street scenes build in speed and frustration, and Volpone's gaiety increase with each encounter. The pace of the action is becoming more intense. The sequence of insults and the predictable reactions are preliminaries to the courtroom solution.

ACT V – SCENE 8

Summary

Volpone encounters Corbaccio and Corvino. He tells them that Mosca has a cozening nose. He expresses surprise that such a witty group could be fooled by a parasite. After a parting remark about the valor of cuckolds, Volpone gleefully escapes the gulls' reach.

Commentary

Volpone has had much fun at the expense of these fools, but the time is fast approaching when he will have to share their burden. As we begin the next scene, Volpone is still disguised as a police officer. It is an excellent excuse for his being in the courtroom. We have encountered all of the principal figures on the way to the courtroon. Let us join them there.

ACT V – SCENE 9

Summary

Just before their arrival at the Senate chamber, Volpone and Voltore meet once more. Volpone tells the vulture that he must be the heir; it is not within the wit of man to cozen so great a lawyer. Volpone is hounded into the courtroom by the seething gulls.

Commentary

These fast, sketchlike scenes are akin to music-hall blackouts. They are short evocations of exaggerated frustration by the plot's key characters. The character actors indicate their growing anger by bulging their eyes, bouncing back and forth on their feet, and with constant, agitated motion of all parts of their bodies, until they suddenly take out after their tormentor. This sort of slapstick is currently employed by all burlesque comedians.

ACT V – SCENE 10

Summary

The whole cast is now assembled at the Senate to play out the game. Just as sentence is about to be pronounced on Bonario and Celia, Voltore interrupts the proceedings. He pleads for mercy to conquer justice. Then Voltore throws himself at the feet of Bonario and Celia and asks their pardon. Pointing to Mosca, Voltore speaks these accusing words: "That parasite, that knave, hath been the instrument of all." In the fuss, Volpone sneaks away into the city. Corvino tries to discredit Voltore's confession by referring to his disappointment in Volpone's will. The court is shocked at the news of Volpone's demise. Voltore clears Volpone of any guilt, but he presents papers that will incriminate Mosca. The court is confused, Bonario is heartened, and Corvino and Corbaccio are in a state of shock. The court, hearing that Mosca is the heir, summons him to appear with the respect due a man of means. Voltore, during the confusion of the courtroom, pushes his papers in front of the *avocatori*.

Commentary

Confusion and chaos now take control of the action. Volpone realizes, too late, the results of his foolish pranks. Voltore's change of heart is not the result of a sickened conscience, nor is it the mere product of the desire to assuage his frustration or to put Mosca in his servant's place. By acquitting Volpone of any guilt in this mess, Voltore still hopes to salvage the fox's fortune for himself. After all, he is the only gull who has done nothing that is publicly punishable. To be sure, he did plead an unjust cause before this very court, but does not every lawyer try to win the case assigned him?

Volpone leaves the court, unnoticed and in despair, having no idea of the depth of his troubles. He realizes that he has been caught in his own noose, but there is always the inventive Mosca to rely upon in such circumstances. At any rate, the scene concludes with matters in a state of confusion.

ACT V – SCENE 11

Summary

Volpone is discovered wandering in the street in a fearful state. "When I had newly 'scaped, was free and clear!" cries the trapped fox. "Out of mere wantonness!" At that moment the three fools come upon the disguised Volpone, who asks them why they are not at home. When he discovers that Mosca has dismissed them, he understands the full extent of his danger. Volpone resolves to try to unscramble the mess by raising Voltore's hopes anew. He instructs the fools to find Mosca and send him to the court.

Commentary

Volpone has finally grasped the extent of his danger and has decided upon a course of action that does not depend upon Mosca. This is his first mistake; the will has placed Volpone in Mosca's hands. Since Volpone has escaped from so many tight places, the audience might still expect him to pull it off once more, but not without the aid and support of Mosca. The two are invincible only when they stand together.

It is important to note that these last scenes have gone from the courtroom to the street and back to the courtroom in rapid succession. This involves moving props and actors at great speed in order to maintain the momentum of the action. It is an indication of the flexibility of the Elizabethan stage and Jonson's grasp of the values of such mobility.

ACT V – SCENE 12

Summary

The court is amazed at the content of the papers presented by Voltore. That Corvino could present his own wife to Volpone seems beyond belief. Celia believes heaven has heard her prayers. Corvino claims that Voltore is angry about the lost inheritance. Volpone, in disguise, returns with the news that Mosca will arrive directly.

Volpone drags Voltore aside and says that Mosca has instructed him to inform the vulture that Volpone lives: it has all been a joke to test Voltore's firmness. Voltore cries out at his own indiscreet violence, whereupon Volpone tells him to feign possession by the devil. Corvino and Corbaccio have accused him of harboring a devil, so why not pretend the devil is in him? Immediately, Voltore collapses to the floor! The court again dissolves into confusion; Volpone stands over the prostrate Voltore, chanting an incantation of possession. Corvino and Corbaccio seize the opportunity to protect their own causes. Suddenly, Voltore innocently comes to himself, asking, "Where am I?" Volpone and the gulls are sympathetic; the court is overwhelmed.

Voltore denies his former pleas that Mosca is a villain. Furthermore, he disputes the report of Volpone's death. At that point, Mosca enters, clad as the heir of Volpone. One of the *avocatori* thinks Mosca a fit man for his daughter, provided Volpone is really dead. Volpone desperately tries to tell Mosca the state of things. Mosca brushes him aside as a knave. The gadfly tells the court that he intends to bury his former master like a gentleman. Volpone, in an aside to the audience, remarks that the body will be cozened and alive. The court does not know what to believe. Mosca, taking advantage of the confusion, bargains with Volpone for half of the fox's fortune. At first, Volpone is unresponsive to this kind of talk. Nonetheless, under the pressure of events, he agrees to the terms. Mosca ups the price immediately. The court asks Voltore who gave him the information that Volpone still lives. Voltore points to the disguised Volpone, who points to Mosca. With great disdain, Mosca denies knowledge of the man. The court orders the disguised Volpone whipped. Volpone will lose his wealth and freedom no matter which way he turns. Consequently, he turns upon Mosca.

Volpone unmasks himself and disregards Mosca's sudden willingness to negotiate. Volpone identifies the gulls and his fellow rogue, Mosca. Everyone's guilt is swiftly established. There is nothing left to do but pass sentence on these fools.

Because Mosca is without noble blood, his sentence is to be a perpetual prisoner in the galleys of Venice. Volpone's substance is given to the hospital for incurables, and he is to be put in chains till he be "sick and lame indeed." Voltore is banished; Corbaccio's estate is given to his son and he goes into a monastery; Corvino will be rowed about Venice with a cap of ass's ears instead of horns. Celia is given treble her dowry and returned to her father.

Volpone steps to the front of the stage and, in a short epilogue, asks for the approbation of the audience.

Commentary

The scene begins with the *avocatori* investigating the papers put into their hands by Voltore. They appear to be so incriminating that no last-minute action by Volpone will stay the hand of disaster. However, when Volpone suggests possession by the devil, Voltore, always the great performer, falls into a faint. Much good theatrical fun can be gained from this sequence by experienced comics. Voltore's sudden recovery, almost without the proper theatrical transition, must be carefully timed. The cliché "Where am I?" is impossible to believe, but the *avocatori* never doubt the vulture's sincerity.

Jonson continues to mock the *avocatori*. The irony of Mosca's eligibility as a son-in-law to a judge as long as he is Volpone's heir is another cut at the courts.

Asides are used more extensively in this sequence than anywhere else in the play. Voltore and Volpone conduct business together at the beginning of the scene, and Volpone and Mosca try to bargain before the unmasking. In the confusion of this scene, it takes great control to move and speak at the exact moment. If the tension is to be maintained, the execution of the performers must be fast and precise.

Finally, when Volpone realizes the jig is up, he melodramatically reveals himself. This is the result of Volpone's judgment of alternative actions. He can keep quiet and escape with a whipping and without money. Mosca will be the master and he will be the parasite. Mosca makes the mistake of thinking that this is an acceptable choice to Volpone. Mosca errs in character judgment because he wants all of the money for himself. He becomes greedy and thereby loses his perspective. Mosca was invincible as long as he was a parasite, but when it becomes possible for him to realize his ambition, his human nature comes to the front. It is this, not the intelligence of the courts, that brings him down. Jonson does not leave the punishment to the courts alone. The failure of a ruse conceived by these two consummate artists is comic punishment; they are their own executioners. It is an irony that is not wasted upon either of them.

So, Volpone, estimating the cost and the satisfaction of revenge, determines to pay the price and pull down his betrayer. It is not an easy decision, and Mosca's desire to negotiate cannot reverse it. In fact, Volpone rather enjoys it because it puts Mosca back under his control. It is Volpone's final irony.

There has been much discussion about the harshness of the court's punishment. The theory is that, in a comedy, such harsh judgment takes the edge off the humor. Jonson has been called a moralist because of the fate he assigned Mosca and Volpone. Some critics feel that these sentences are in keeping with the stupidity of the judges, though they are out of proportion to the offenses. Others feel that the conclusion represents the symbolic flagellation and death of a god or prince of fools, who must at all costs be kept under control.

It might be well to remember the sentence of banishment from the court of Henry V meted out to another roguish comic figure, Falstaff. Furthermore, there is much evidence to suggest that Elizabethans were not averse to having their comedy and tragedy mixed into one package. Shakespeare's audiences appear to have enjoyed the Machiavellian villainy of Richard III and Iago. Much of the work of these two characters has been made uproariously funny by great actors. Are these plays to be condemned for making people laugh when they are essentially serious works?

Finally, Jonson was writing a comedy from a foreign model, while most of his contemporaries were writing festival comedy along sentimental lines. There was no precedent in English comedy for this kind of work, and Jonson had to play his methods by ear. There can be little doubt that our time does not appreciate the worth of this play. But it is not simply because of the harsh ending. It is probably a result of the cruelty in the picture of human greed, and the unflinching willingness to face the harsh facts of human nature. Sentimentality does not figure in *Volpone*. Even the hero and heroine are silly fools. The twentieth-century desire to identify with a character in a play makes it difficult for this one to please. Most people can identify with certain character qualities of a fool, but few people are criminal in their folly.

One critic has written that Volpone almost becomes human and that the sentence is leveled against a human rather than a comic character. At any rate, Jonson has been able to bring *Volpone* to life for the stage.

CHARACTER ANALYSIS

VOLPONE

Volpone (the fox) is the central figure of the play. He begins the action by his plots and intrigues, and it is the audience's interest in the manner of his downfall that preserves the dramatic tension until the final curtain.

Volpone, as the name suggests, is a simple dramatic character. He is a trickster who delights in disguises and intrigues. His actions are complicated in plot but simple in the psychology of the character that executes them. Volpone loves to trick people into giving him their most prized possessions. When he has secured these through cunning rather than ordinary means, the value is increased in the fox's eyes. In short, his character treasures the chagrin of those he has cozened more than the wealth received as a result of the cozening.

There is excellent comic sense in the simplicity and single-mindedness of Volpone's character. His insatiable desire to trick people is characteristic of the figure of the fool. Volpone is a nobleman, but he shares the same human nature as the lowly fools of his household. They are naturally deformed; Volpone is the cause of his own deformation. The plot shows his fall from the position of Venetian nobleman to the social position of a fool. Volpone's character flaw, the desire to trick people, has brought him to the final curtain. He starts out playing the fool and ends up by being one. He fulfills Mosca's prescription of people: "Almost all the wise world is little else, in nature, but parasites or sub-parasites."

MOSCA

Mosca (the gadfly) is a parasite; this bestiary name encompasses the simple character of Volpone's servant. Mosca is only one step higher in the social scale than the three deformed fools of Volpone's household: the dwarf, the hermaphrodite, and the eunuch. He is socially deformed, a fellow of no birth or blood.

Mosca lives by his wits; he has no possibility of advancement in the Venetian world and he is therefore free of the folly of greed. He takes his needs from the treasures of others, and he takes only his daily needs.

The parasite's freedom from the normal ambitions of human nature makes him a formidable judge of it. He uses this knowledge to mock the frailties of his fellow men, and his only pleasure is in his wise observance that, if he is not noble, they are parasites. It is only when Volpone's need for cozening puts the weapon of financial advancement into Mosca's hands that the gadfly tries to live by his own means. Mosca's sudden opportunity for gain makes him vulnerable to the folly of greed, which eventually pulls down the charming and inventive rogue. This comic character flaw is particularly ironic in Mosca; it is the very folly he has been so delightfully mocking for five acts. Did he for a moment forget that "almost all the wise world is little else, in nature, but parasites or sub-parasites"?

VOLTORE

The vulture is one of the three birds of prey that circle around the fox, greedy and full of expectation. He is a lawyer and consequently has a weakness for wills. He uses his legal knowledge to advocate injustice in order to possess Volpone's fortune. Mosca wisely fools this gull by employing the advocate's own tactics; that is, he tells Voltore the biggest lie and documents it with elements of well-known facts.

Voltore is tricked by his own folly. He can, he believes, with quick agility, make the wide world believe that a lie is the truth. He fails to observe that he, as part of the wide world, might be cozened himself.

CORBACCIO

The carrion crow is old and decrepit, deaf, round of back, and very avaricious. Partially deformed by old age, this fool completes his transformation from nobleman to parasite by being tricked into disinheriting his son.

The irony of Corbaccio's spiritual condition is wrapped up in his physical condition: he really expects to outlive Volpone and inherit his wealth! This comic character flaw is not physical blindness but spiritual blindness.

CORVINO

The raven is the last of the greedy trio, a peacock proud of his beauty, Celia. This bird of prey is an exceedingly jealous husband who guards his wife with great care. Nonetheless, his greed persuades him to demand that Volpone cuckold him! When at last he discovers the error of his ways, he is too proud to reveal his foolish vanity. The paramount character quality of the three divergent birds of prey is their love and desire to possess money.

CELIA AND BONARIO

Celia is that ripe beauty, Corvino's wife; she is also an important plot device. It is Volpone's desire that delivers her to his doorstep. Her presence there gives Bonario a chance to save her.

Bonario is the good fellow of the play; he is also sentimentally romantic. Celia and Bonario are foolish as well as innocent. They look at life in Venice through the eyes of lovers of melodramatic, romantic fiction. Therefore, they are not human beings who suffer through uncontrollable circumstances. Rather, they seriously misjudge the people they should know best, because of their naive ideas about human nature.

If the gulls seem inhuman in their total greed, Bonario and Celia are equally inhuman in their purity. Their folly is more silly than vicious, but it is, nonetheless, folly.

SIR POLITIC AND LADY WOULD-BE AND PEREGRINE

Sir Politic, his wife, Lady Would-be, and Peregrine are travelers from England. Sir Pol and his lady are English tourists trying to go native. They are hilariously inept at playing Italian games and hopelessly ignorant of the ways of the foreigners. They are parrots mimicking the action of the master plotters without ever understanding what they are doing. Underneath it all, they are innocent and stupid, but likable and English.

Peregrine serves as Sir Politic's confidant. He uses the English knight for his merriment but never becomes involved in the main action of the play.

REVIEW QUESTIONS

1. What is the function of the Sir Politic Would-be — Peregrine subplot?
2. What is the dramatic significance of the animal names of Volpone, Mosca, and the three birds of prey?
3. Give an example of implied physical movement and stage fun in the dialogue of the play.
4. Explain Mosca's statement that "almost all the wise world is little else, in nature, but parasites or sub-parasites."
5. What dramatic comic value did Jonson hope to suggest by using the characters of Nano, Androgyno, and Castrone?
6. Give an example of the use of hyperbole to promote dramatic irony in the play.
7. Is Celia's virtue a comic parody, or is it dramatically convincing? Explain.
8. How does the scene-shifting of the last act demonstrate the flexibility of the Elizabethan stage?
9. Why does Volpone throw off his disguise in the last scene?

10. What causes Mosca's sudden failure to understand Volpone's nature in the last scene? Explain.

11. Is the punishment of the company a comic or moral one? Explain.

ESSAY TOPICS

1. Compare Jacques' statement in Shakespeare's *As You Like It* that all the world's a stage with Mosca's that all the world is little else but parasites.

2. Compare Niccolò Machiavelli's *The Mandrake* to *Volpone*.

3. Compare the savage irony of Jonson's hyperbole and the harsh ending of Volpone with the same elements in Molière's *Tartuffe*.

4. Describe Mosca's physical appearance, age, and voice and support your casting with textual references. Contrast this exercise with a similar one of Volpone.

The Alchemist Notes

ALCHEMY AND ALLIED ARTS

The modern reader is sometimes confused by the importance of alchemy in this play. Obviously Jonson does not believe in alchemy, and the reader does not readily accept the idea that others were taken in by so implausible a swindle. In addition, he is confused by the terminology. He has difficulty following Jacobean English at the best of times, and now he is doubly confused by the elaborate jargon that he finds wholly improbable.

Actually by the use of alchemy Jonson added additional specific satire to his play. Alchemy was taken seriously by many people at the time; many who did not believe it maintained an open mind on the subject—a form of nonsense only slightly less reprehensible. Monarchs employed alchemists, and alchemists did succeed in swindling great sums of money from people otherwise considered sagacious. In 1565 Queen Elizabeth hired an alchemist who was supposed to produce 50,000 crowns a year. He did not succeed and was confined to the Tower, where he probably died. In 1604, very close to the time of the play, a Scottish alchemist, Seton, apparently managed to convince many people of scientific bent of mind that he *had* succeeded. The names of Dee and Kelley are so famous in the history of alchemy in England that a book published in 1668 assumed that *The Alchemist* contained personal satire directed at them. Dr. Simon Foreman, a practitioner of alchemy and the allied arts, was thriving in 1610 (he died in 1611). Sir Francis Bacon still felt it necessary to render alchemy the deference of serious refutation in *Sylva Sylvanum*, one of his Latin philosophical works.

It is difficult to know whether alchemists at the time were their own dupes or not. Of Subtle we might say that he had at one time believed, for certainly he is a very learned man in the field. And for Subtle to be learned, Jonson, too, must have studied the art; he could not write into the play knowledge he did not have. Modern scholarship, indefatigable in the pursuit of truth, has ascertained that Jonson's knowledge is sound and thorough. Subtle's debate with Surly in Act II supplies us with the rationale for the pseudo-science, a blend of false analogies wholly plausible to those who would believe. The alchemist's arguments were borrowed from a book Jonson used frequently, *Disquitiones Magicae* by Martin Delrio. Neither the title nor the author is very important for us; what is relevant is that the date of publication was 1599-1600.

That the science could continue so long despite obvious repeated failures would appear to be due to two factors. There were always rumors of those who had succeeded, in another place or at another time. Ananias in Act III supplied us with one such rumor. In addition, the alchemist had his justifications for failure incorporated in the requirements of the science. Not only were the processes very complicated and the technical requirements very precise, but the practice of alchemy also required complete morality amounting to saintliness (even of thought) of those engaged in it. A swindler could always depend on some flaw in the procedure or on someone's deviating from this strict morality, at least in thought. Mammon can believe that his impure thoughts were the reason that the procedure failed, not that the quest was impossible in the first place. This, of course, accounts for the holy man guise adopted by Subtle in his dealings with Mammon.

Perhaps even more implausible for the modern reader are the Dapper-Queen of Fairy episodes. They seem to be entirely outside the bounds of reason. Court records of 1605-10 describe a fraud: a man was promised an introduction to the Queen of Fairy, whom he would marry! There are records of similar episodes in the years after the presentation of *The Alchemist*. It is no reflection on Jonson's originality to say that England supplied ample absurdities on which to exercise his imagination.

The reader may also be confused by other skills to which Subtle lays claim in his swindles. The alchemist was likely to be an astrologer and a doctor. He would also read omens, be a master of the symbolism of signs, be skilled in divination, and possibly also be a necromancer. In all the swindles in which the learned doctor is engaged, he is professing knowledge that would at the time be incorporated in one practitioner.

LIST OF CHARACTERS

Face (Jeremy)

A member of the trio of conspirators. He is actually Jeremy, the butler of the Lovewit household, whom his master left in charge during an outbreak of the plague in London. He recruited two others who now use the house as a base of operations while swindling, it appears, a substantial part of the London population.

Subtle

Another member of the trio of conspirators. He was an alchemist, thoroughly trained in his art, but unfortunately destitute when Face discovered him and they formed their partnership.

Dol Common

The third member of the trio of conspirators. She was Subtle's doxy when they met with Face and went into partnership.

Dapper

One of the conspirators' victims. He is a lawyer's clerk who wants to be lucky in gambling. A stupid and greedy young man, he is easy game for the swindlers.

Drugger

Another of the conspirators' customers. A tobacconist who is planning to open a shop, he wants advice on the luckiest way to orient his shop and merchandise.

Sir Epicure Mammon

The most lucrative of the firm's customers. He is a man with dreams of power, riches, and luxury. For some months he has been subsidizing Subtle's pretended efforts to produce the philosopher's stone.

Pertinax Surly

A friend of Mammon. A poor gentleman himself, he is not fooled by the tricksters. He sets a trap to expose them.

Ananias

A member of the sect of Anabaptists (i.e., a Puritan), he too is a customer of Subtle's. The Puritans want the philosopher's stone because they need money for the activities of the sect.

Tribulation Wholesome

Also a Puritan, and the pastor of the congregation. There is a strong hint that he may have more selfish reasons for wanting the stone than just the good of the Puritans.

Kastrill

A young man who inherited wealth and came to London. He wants to learn to quarrel fashionably and live by his wits.

Dame Pliant

The sister of Kastrill, a wealthy and beautiful young widow who is not overly bright. She becomes the center of a number of intrigues, for many men want to marry her.

Lovewit

The master of the house, whose unexpected return upsets all the well laid plans of the swindlers.

Neighbors, Constables, etc.

PLOT SUMMARY

Lovewit, a London gentleman, left London during an outbreak of the plague, entrusting his spacious home to the care of a butler or "housekeeper," Jeremy. Jeremy, a man of greater enterprise than his master realized, found an alchemist, Subtle, and his woman confederate, Dol Common, who were at the moment destitute. The three of them pooled their meager resources and considerable talents to swindle the gullible, using the Lovewit mansion as their base of operations.

As the opening scene indicates, the partnership has problems. There is internal dissension. Each of the men feels he has made the greater contribution to the group treasury and wants more than the originally agreed-upon share. Dol has the job of keeping the two men from taking ruinous actions in their pique. She manages to end the present quarrel just as their first client of the day arrives.

The basis of the operation is this: Subtle is a skilled alchemist, an astrologer, and a palm and face reader; he is also, of course, a charlatan in all of these areas. Face, sometimes disguised as a captain, plays the part of a man-about-town and recruits customers for Subtle's services. As needed, he wears other disguises.

Dol Common assists when their schemes require feminine help, occasionally engaging in prostitution, presumably her regular profession. In the course of the next little time, the clients appear. Dapper, a young man who wants a charm to make him lucky in gambling, arrives. He is encouraged to escalate his desires, for, says Subtle, the young man is blessed with good fortune through his aunt, the Queen of Fairy! Dapper leaves to bring more money.

Next appears Drugger, a tobacconist who is seeking help in opening a new shop. He wants his horoscope read, advice on the right orientation of his merchandise, and the lucky sign for his establishment.

An old client, Sir Epicure Mammon, a man with wild orgiastic dreams now arrives with a friend, Surly. Mammon has commissioned Subtle to manufacture the philosopher's stone. With him Subtle plays the part of the very pious scholar while Face is the apprentice alchemist. They promise Mammon the philosopher's stone very shortly—provided he maintain purity of thought and nobility of intent. To enmesh him further, they permit him to see Dol, presumably accidentally, whom they describe as a lord's sister who has gone mad on the subject of theology; in all other matters she is sane. Face promises to help Mammon woo her. But Surly is not convinced, and the appearance of Dol makes him certain that the men are swindlers; among other things, the establishment is a bawdy house. He makes plans to expose the plotters.

After Mammon leaves, promising Face (as servant) to woo Dol later, another client arrives, Ananias, representing the Puritans who also want the philosopher's stone. Subtle treats Ananias roughly when he hears that the Puritans will supply no more money until they see some results. Drugger now appears, and Face (disguised as the captain) assures him of future success. When Drugger tells them of a young, green, wealthy squire who has, together with his wealthy widowed sister, come to town, Face induces Drugger to bring them to the doctor and encourages Drugger to believe that he may marry the wealthy, young, and beautiful widow.

Since the entire play covers only one day, the action now speeds up. Ananias and his pastor, Tribulation, arrive. Subtle convinces them of the efficacy of his art and talks them into continuing to support the researches. He points out that he can turn pewter into Dutch dollars. They leave to consider a fine point of law — coining is illegal, but perhaps "casting" of coins is not.

Face, who has been out, reports the acquisition of a new customer for Dol. He is a Spanish count who has just arrived in London. Dapper arrives to be introduced to his aunt, the Queen of Fairy, a part to be played by Dol, but they are interrupted as Drugger returns with his friend Kastrill. Kastrill is so convinced that Subtle can teach the art of quarreling like a gentleman that he leaves to bring his sister. As the conspirators blindfold Dapper to prepare him to meet his aunt, they are again interrupted, this time by Mammon. Dapper is hustled, blindfolded and gagged, into the privy.

Mammon and Dol are in turn interrupted and whisked into another room when Kastrill and Dame Pliant arrive. Subtle, among his many talents, is a skillful matchmaker, and Kastrill is quite prepared to leave his sister's future in the wise man's hands. Subtle and Face, not surprisingly, plan to snare the fortune, but since each wants to marry the heiress, they quarrel again.

When the Spanish count, actually Surly in disguise, arrives, the cheaters are for a moment caught unprepared, for Dol is occupied with Mammon. They therefore decide to trick Dame Pliant into substituting for Dol, pretending that Subtle forecasts her marriage to a Spanish count. Obviously they do not assume that the count has any intention of marrying a woman whom he believes to be a prostitute. They leave her with Surly in yet another part of the house. The partners quarrel over Dame Pliant again, but now each is anxious that the other marry her.

Mammon's courtship of the mentally-ill lord's sister proceeds according to plan. Inevitably the knight says something that triggers Dol's fit. This is the excuse Subtle has been waiting for.

Just after he accuses Mammon of carnal intent, an explosion occurs—the entire work is destroyed because of Mammon's sinfulness! Mammon's gulling has now been completed.

The Surly-Dame Pliant affair, however, does not proceed as anticipated. Surly exposes the swindlers' plot; what he did not guess before he overheard as they talked before the Spanish Don, who knew no English. He proposes marriage, pointing out the gratitude she should feel for him. But when he confronts Subtle, the plotters, to his surprise, are equal to the occasion. As each of the other gulls enters, Face enlists him against Surly: Kastril is obviously eager enough to quarrel; Drugger knows that Surly is his debtor in his shop; Ananias sees in Surly's Spanish dress the ultimate abomination. And Surly is driven off by the very people whom he would help.

The activities of the combine are brought to a sudden end by the return of Lovewit, Face's master and the owner of the house. Neighbors tell Lovewit of the strange people who have been coming to the house. Face now dresses as Jeremy, the butler (whom no one has seen for some months), and tries to convince Lovewit that the neighbors are lying. Unfortunately, the swindlers forget about Dapper, who has managed to rid himself of his gag, and when he calls out, Jeremy can only confess the whole affair. Lovewit, who dearly loves a joke, forgives his servant completely, especially since Jeremy promises him the accumulated loot and a young and beautiful heiress as a wife. To save himself, therefore, Jeremy cheats his partners, just a few minutes before they are able to cheat him.

Lovewit's marriage with Dame Pliant is immediately contracted; but he has still to earn the booty and his bride, for now the entire group of gulls arrive, Mammon and Surly with police, Kastrill to fight, the Puritans for their goods. Lovewit turns each of them off in turn: he is willing to return to Mammon whatever of his property is left—if he will procure a warrant from the police; to do this Mammon would have to admit his gullibility. He chases off the others, and he out-blusters the angry boy, Kastrill, who loves him for it. At the play's end, Lovewit alone has profited. Face, Subtle, and Dol are left exactly where they were at the beginning of their conspiracy. Face is again Jeremy, the butler; Subtle and Dol are penniless vagrants wandering somewhere about the streets of London.

SUMMARIES AND COMMENTARIES

NOTE: The division into acts and scenes followed in this section is based on the *Mermaid Dramabook* edition (see Bibliography). However, other editions indicate a new scene, as the French dramatists did, almost every time a character enters or leaves the stage. This practice was presumably based on classical instructions. There were, of course, no breaks in the performance of the play. The *Mermaid Dramabook* is consistent with standard English practice. The scenes (French style) covered in each unit of the Summaries and Commentaries are noted. For instance, the heading ACT III—SCENE 2 (III—2-5) indicates that the material in Act III, Scene 2 of the *Mermaid Dramabook* includes Scenes 2 through 5 in editions that follow the French practice.

DEDICATION

"To the Lady Most Deserving Her Name and Blood, Lady Mary Wroth."

Commentary

This dedication is short. Modern readers consider it in better taste than others of the period, which were often composed of fulsome praise. In fact, in the last sentence Jonson makes the point that to continue praise would make the dedication seem artificial.

TO THE READER

Commentary

Jonson expresses dissatisfaction with much of the drama of the time. There is a "concupiscence of dances and of antics." The plays are ill constructed, and if there are good things in them, it is only because everything is thrown into them; inevitably there are some successful bits, even if only by chance. His moral is in the last sentence: "For it is only the disease of the unskillful to think rude things greater than polished."

PROLOGUE

Commentary

The person interested in the handling of verse might examine this prologue with care. The lines resemble heroic couplets, but they are quite different in their impact. The ideas expressed do not fall into two-line units; they do not depend upon balanced rhythms and antithesis of ideas. The grammatical periods are not in normal English order. The first two and a half lines can illustrate. The normal arrangement would be approximately this: "Judging spectators, for both your sake and ours, we wish away [i.e., magically caused to disappear] Fortune, which [usually] favors fools."

Jonson makes some interesting points. He calls attention to the fact that his play is set in London rather than in some exotic never-never land; in that sense it is realistic. He makes the implication explicit, that England has its own share of bawds, squires (i.e., pimps), imposters, and generally people of humour. He further makes the point that many will see themselves mirrored—although they may not acknowledge that these are their own follies.

ARGUMENT

Commentary

It does not appear that "The Argument" was delivered at any production; there is already a prologue which states the plot of the play briefly. "The Argument," like the one prepared for *Volpone*, is in the form of an acrostic, a stunt that had appeal at the time it was written. These acrostics imitate the lines added by later writers to the plays of Plautus.

ACT I
(I – 1-4)

Summary

The play opens in the middle of a quarrel between Subtle and Face which Dol Common is anxiously trying to quiet. The conspirators are apparently so angry with each other that they are ready to reveal their activities to the police out of spite. In the course of the argument we learn that Face was a "housekeeper," a superior liveried servant, Subtle, a starving vagabond, unable to make even the simplest living by the practice of alchemy. Face supplied his employer's house as headquarters for the combine's operations while the owner, Lovewit, is absent from London to avoid the plague. Each of the men is certain that his is the greater contribution to the prosperity of the group. After considerable effort, Dol manages to impose some common sense; grumbling, the conspirators agree to work together for their common good and society's peril.

The first of the day's visitors arrives: Dapper, a lawyer's clerk whom Face, disguised as a captain, met the night before at a tavern. Dapper wants a familiar spirit to help him in his gambling. Subtle pretends to be very hesitant about arranging for such a spirit, for it is against the law, obviously the right tone to take when dealing with a law clerk. Face pretends anger that the doctor will not accommodate his newfound friend and insists that Subtle take the money offered by Dapper. Only to accommodate Face, Subtle accepts the fee.

Now, however, Dapper increases his modest request for a familiar that might be of occasional help to something that would make him an all-powerful gambler—and Face proceeds to raise the price. Subtle assures Dapper that his art informs him of the young man's noble future. He will indeed be a very fortunate gambler, for he is related to the Queen of Fairy. She will help Dapper, but first there are many ceremonies to perform. Of course, Face points out the client must fee the doctor further. As there is a knock at the door, Dapper is led off to make room for the next cully. In the meantime, he is advised to bring with him some "twenty nobles" for distribution to the Queen of Fairy's retinue.

Abel Drugger is a tobacconist, "free of the grocers." He, too, was recruited by the captain. Drugger's wants are simple. Since he is about to open a tobacco shop, he seeks advice from Subtle on the lucky orientation of his door and shelves. Once again, merely by looking at him, Subtle can see that Drugger will rise rapidly in the guild of grocers, and he tells him where to place his door and shelves. Face now takes over, and while Drugger wanted to give Subtle a crown, wheedles a portague (about 14 crowns). Drugger leaves after requesting that the doctor check his almanac and mark his unlucky days.

Sir Epicure Mammon is on the way. Mammon is the firm's biggest customer. For him Subtle has been preparing the philosopher's stone, and for the last few days Sir Epicure has been acting as if the stone were already in his possession.

Commentary

The act falls into three parts: the quarrel between the conspirators, followed by two passages that show Subtle and Face cooperating to cheat their victims. The quarrel is itself interesting.

The acting of the scene is discussed elsewhere, but we may mention here that the actors' movements about the stage have elements of both a duel and a comic choreography. Exposition and preparation are both effective. We are informed of what happened and the eventual breakdown of the highly imaginative enterprise is forecasted.

The theme of avarice is presented doubly: the men who exploit the avarice of others understand avarice well, for it is their vice also, and they will eventually be their own victims. Dol Common alone shows a sensible attitude in her chicanery.

Disguise has both comic and symbolic value. It not only imposes on the outsider, but it imposes on the wearer as well. Subtle is angry in quite an unmonk-like way (he is not wearing the alchemist's robe). Face's show of anger is consistent with the captain's role he is at the moment playing.

Subtle's language in talking to Face is noteworthy. The alchemy he uses to defraud is his natural way of thought, and therefore speech: "have I ta'en thee out of dung/.... *Sublimed* thee, and *exalted* thee... to *spirit*, to *quintessence*...." Ironically, the transmutation in Face's fortunes will prove as spurious as the transmutation alchemy effects in any other area.

It is dramatically useful to observe how Dapper and Drugger are manipulated. Dapper is treated contemptuously. He is easy game, succumbing to any devices, led by his avarice, on which the swindlers play. At first he hopes only for a familiar to help him in some cautious gambling, but he is encouraged to grow in avarice as Subtle talks of great success. He is mulcted for additional money, and he has left himself open for a series of humiliating experiences. He is manhandled and abused, for he has neither the intelligence nor the courage to resent indignity.

Drugger is also an easy victim, relatively modest in his demands. A naive and comic figure, we can laugh at him with superiority and condescension. Face acts to raise his contribution, while Subtle plays the part of the man who is indifferent to money.

The arrival of Sir Epicure is prepared for with some fanfare, for he is the most important of the victims.

ACT II
(II – 1-6)

Summary

Sir Epicure Mammon and Surly arrive. Sir Epicure, who believes that Subtle will soon succeed in producing the philosopher's stone, is apostrophizing alchemy, gold, and his own future. The philosopher's stone will not only turn base metals to gold, but will restore health and youth. Surly, however, is highly skeptical; he will believe only when he is shown. Sir Epicure becomes increasingly insistent in his efforts to convince his friend, finally blurting out that Adam wrote a book on alchemy – in "High Dutch," thus solving the vexed problem of what language our first father spoke.

Face enters disguised as a servant, or, we might say, a sorcerer's apprentice. He reports optimistically on the state of the philosopher's stone. Color, heat, and so on are all correct; one can expect "projection" shortly. (His name in this capacity is Ulen Spiegel, although Sir Epicure delights in calling him "Lungs" – i.e., he who works the bellows.) Subtle, we are informed, is at his prayers, for devotion on the part of the practitioner is one of the requirements for the success of alchemy. In a number of long speeches Sir Epicure describes the good, rich, and full life he intends to lead as soon as Subtle has supplied him with the stone. Lungs is suitably impressed and successfully plays the part of a servitor simple enough to go through the trials and tribulations of his craft to supply the stone for someone else's use.

Subtle enters. He has donned a monk's robe, or some similar garment, and a benign manner to match. He chides the knight gently, for Sir Epicure's eagerness suggests "carnal appetite." Since carnal appetite may result in the destruction of the process, Subtle is preparing Mammon for the failure of the project. There ensues a set of instructions to Face, all concerned with the fine details of the process. Mammon is tremendously impressed, but Surly, made acute by suspicion, hears talk of "the work wants something." This, he feels, correctly, is preparation for later failure of the project. By the end of the speech, Sir Epicure has been mulcted for an additional ten pounds and is ready to send out more brass, pewter, and iron stuff, all of which will be transformed into gold.

Subtle's explanation, to Surly, of the validity of the alchemical art has the appearance of sweet reasonableness and clear logic. Surly is out-argued, although he is not convinced; Sir Epicure, however, is ecstatic.

Now further bait is introduced. Dol appears suddenly to provide Lungs with the excuse to tell Mammon that she is "a lord's sister" who has gone mad "with studying Broughton's works." She is there to be cured, for the ability to work strange cures is another of Subtle's talents. Surly is now certain that these are confidence men, and "this is a bawdy house." Mammon is so completely convinced that he even pretends to know the lord.

When "Lungs" returns, he tells Surly that Captain Face has left a message that he wants to meet Surly in town. The mention of Face is further assurance for Surly of his suspicions, for he knows that "Captain" Face is a scoundrel and a pimp. Lungs promises Mammon to further his cause with the sister of the lord.

As the three conspirators gloat over their progress with Mammon, a new client arrives. Subtle immediately rids himself of his robe, for he presents a different temperament to the "Anabaptist" Ananias. He is now angry and bullying. The Anabaptists are to buy some of the goods which Mammon will bring, for they, in turn, want them turned to gold. But Ananias makes clear that they will not underwrite any further research until they see some results. Subtle now pretends a violent rage and refuses to deal with a man whose name is Ananias. He gives the

Puritans sixty minutes to appear, for if they do not, the entire brew will be destroyed.

After he leaves, Face (now again Captain) returns with Drugger, who brings more gold. Subtle indicates that he has been working on a lucky sign for the shop. Drugger tells them of a young wealthy widow lately come to town with a brother, also young, who would "learn to quarrel, and to live by his wits." Face points out that Subtle is an expert on the proper art of quarreling. Drugger is to fetch both brother and sister.

Face and Subtle are delighted with the latest turn of events. They plan that one of them marry the widow for her fortune and divide the money. They agree that this plan must be kept a secret from Dol.

Commentary

The name Sir Epicure Mammon indicates the vices that make up the knight's personality. They are vices that blanket and color others. He wants to surround his approach to food, sexual indulgence, and power with all the appurtenances of wealth and to refine on his lechery. Yet he is not a fool. He is a brilliant example of a very difficult kind of character to create: he deludes himself because he wills to delude himself. He is disgusting yet fascinating as he describes with salacious joy his fantasies of food, lechery, luxurious wealth—all tied to an essentially clearsighted contempt for people. His language is a mirror of his mind, for he thinks in pictorial images that are highly poetic even if frequently repulsive.

The entrance of Surly supplies the first indication of external forces that can destroy the triumvirate; the opening of the play made clear that there was internal dissension. Surly's comment that he has a humour, "I would not willingly be gulled" should be noted.

The first of the major disguise changes appears here. In Act I Face was the Captain, Subtle presumably his own charming self. Here Subtle plays the part of the holy alchemist who not only knows his art but also spends much of his time in prayer. Face is Ulen Spiegel, or Lungs, the sorcerer's apprentice, stupid yet cunning. No matter how Mammon may wish to believe, it would still be necessary for him to see some reason why the alchemist would work to make him, Mammon, rich, and not himself; this reason is supplied.

Jonson made a thorough study of the art of alchemy. The language, the terminology, and the description of the process are all correct. Mammon, who has some learning in the field, although perhaps less than he pretends, is convinced of Subtle's skill and his sincerity. Subtle's discussion with Surly is a clear and convincing defense of the alchemist's art. The sensitivity of the process was a necessary part of the art—for how else could the practitioner explain to his gulls (he was himself frequently the greatest) why the philosopher's stone did not result?

It is no surprise to Mammon that the doctor is curing a woman who has gone mad. The philosopher's stone was actually believed to have all the virtues he described. It could heal all illnesses and win honor, love, respect, and long life; it could restore youth and virility.

When Ananias comes, Subtle changes into a more appropriate costume; for, except for avarice, Subtle has no character, only the many personalities that he assumes. His dupes are hypocrites, but he is hypocrisy itself. A benign manner and the pretense of holiness would be wasted on Puritans. They know that game too well. They must be attacked and overawed, to Subtle's great satisfaction, for he, the arch-hypocrite finds their hypocrisy contemptible!

Ananias, and later his companion, are special objects of Jonson's dislike. There is an ironic touch here that may perhaps need pointing out. Ananias will supply no more money—the brothers have already contributed 120 pounds. At first it appears that this is reasonable caution, even if reason and caution come late. In the next lines we see that good sense is not involved.

There is instead greater gullibility tied to niggardliness even when what the Puritans are buying is unlimited riches: "One at Heidelberg, made it of an egg,/ And a small paper of pin-dust." When Subtle shows off alchemical knowledge to Ananias, he does it harshly, with no recourse to the gentler arts of persuasion.

With Drugger Subtle changes again; he is now a busy man, impatient at the interruption. The sign he has developed for Drugger is a contemptuous trick on the simpleton, as well as a satiric commentary by Jonson on the kinds of punning symbolism common at the time in emblems or shop-board signs.

ACT III – SCENE 1
(III – 1)

Summary

Ananias and Tribulation Wholesome arrive at the house, engaged in conversation. "We must bend unto all means/ That may give furtherance to the holy cause." The end, in other words, justifies the means, an abhorrent position. Consistent with it, he accounts for Subtle's temperament as a (forgivable) result of his profession. "What makes the devil so devilish... but his being/ Perpetually about the fire, and boiling/ Brimstone and arsenic?" As the Puritans need money badly to bribe judges in Amsterdam, they must deal with Subtle. Ananias says, "I have not [been] edified more, truly, by man;/ Not since the beautiful light first shone on me."

This scene introduces Tribulation Wholesome. Tribulation is drawn with a bitterness that reveals Ben Jonson's special hatred for the Puritans. The doctrine that the end justifies the means is Machiavellian, and the argument that Subtle is to be forgiven his bad manners, and, presumably, evil ways, because working with fire would make him devilish is, of course, entirely specious. In the next scene Tribulation reveals his venal opportunism even more clearly.

Ananias is certainly the more naive of the two; he has also some honesty. And it is ironic that, with complete trust in Tribulation, he can say that he has never been "so edified."

ACT III – SCENE 2
(III – 2-5)

Summary

Subtle permits himself to be pacified by Tribulation, who apologizes for Ananias' excessive zeal. The brethren, Subtle is informed, are prepared to buy the metal of the "orphans" (the stuff the conspirators expect to get from Mammon). Subtle describes at length the value of the philosopher's stone. It can rejuvenate old men or women and cure their leprosy or rheumatism to turn them into valuable and powerful friends. With the money the stone would supply, they could discard some of the manners of the Puritans. Throughout, Ananias keeps interrupting as Subtle offends against some point of doctrine. The Puritans leave with promises of success in "eight, nine, ten days hence," after they promise to send more coal.

Before they go, an interesting point of conscience arises. Subtle says he can melt pewter and make good Dutch dollars of it, by the addition of "a tincture." But coining is not lawful; however, "casting of money may be lawful." Tribulation has convinced himself; it is certain he will convince the brethren.

Face, as Captain, now returns, because Surly did not keep his appointment. The trip to town has not been a waste, however. He met instead a wealthy Spanish don who has come secretly to London, and he has arranged for the don to take Subtle's bath (presumably the bath has powers to increase virility or rejuvenate). The don also intends an assignation with Dol. While Face tells Dol to prepare for the Spaniard's visit, Dapper appears. He is now to undergo the ceremony involved in meeting his aunt, the Queen of Fairy. However, Drugger arrives with Kastrill, the young man from the country. Kastrill is loud and obnoxious, a man who wants to learn how to be a bully.

Face glowingly describes the doctor's skill. Not only does Subtle know all the rules of dueling, but he can forecast the results of the encounter with an "instrument." He lauds his partner's other talents: he can teach a man to live by his wits—after he has lost his money; he can make a wealthy man of Dapper, a forty-marks-a-year law clerk (Dapper is still onstage). In addition, Subtle is skillful in arranging matches for rich widows. As he improvises, Face keeps reminding Drugger of the pound of tobacco he was to bring (and did) and the damask he was to bring, but didn't. Kastrill is so impressed that he dashes off for his sister.

Subtle has been using this time to disguise himself as a "priest of Fairy"—and now the gulling and comic humiliation of Dapper proceeds. He is first deprived of all the money he has with him, and then he is made ready to meet his "aunt," a role Dol is to play. As part of the ritual, he is blindfolded with a strip of the Queen's smock. Again they are interrupted, now by Sir Epicure. Face changes from his captain's uniform into the apprentice's clothes, while he talks to the blindfolded Dapper on the one hand and Sir Epicure through the door on the other. Subtle and Dol, in the meantime, gag the bewildered Dapper with a piece of gingerbread, and take him off for a couple of hours to "Fortune's privy lodgings"—a bad pun, for the "lodgings" are the privy, where "the fumigation's somewhat strong."

Commentary

In the preceding act Subtle and Face together manipulated both Mammon and Ananias. In the two most impressive passages in Act III, Subtle and Face act independently. Subtle gulls, cozens, and deludes both Puritans. He maintains the hard, unbending manner he displayed earlier, but lets himself be placated. By the end of the scene the brethren are prepared to wait for ten days; they will bring money for more coal; they will buy (at a good price) the household metals supplied by Sir Epicure; and they are prepared to fetch pewter, for Subtle to turn into good Dutch dollars.

The most revealing single passage is the quibble on coining and casting. The brethren would not coin money (which is against the law), but Tribulation lets himself be convinced that the casting of money is legal: greed is covered by a self-deluding hypocrisy.

Despite the fact that the Puritans are hypocrites, Subtle demonstrates that they are not able to recognize hypocrisy, even when it is spelled out for them. The philosopher's stone, as Subtle suggests, will gain them friends medicinally, as well as the money for power. They will not need to get pious widows to give them legacies or zealous wives to rob their husbands for the cause. They will no longer have to foreclose on debtors. There will be no need for the mummery of fast-days or worry about laws of dress. They need not attack aldermen, or pretend to abhor the theater, or call themselves by odd names, such as Tribulation. All these, implies Subtle, are devices to play upon the gullible. Yet only a few lines later Subtle talks piously of selling the metal goods at the highest price "for conscience' sake." His guests do not recognize the phrase as hypocritical cant, even after he has described the art so thoroughly.

Face arrives, blustering that Surly did not meet him. Yet it is possible that Subtle is the angrier of the two. Face, after all, knows that there is no money to be gained from Surly; Surly is himself too shrewd, and, most important, too poor. Subtle, however, takes obvious delight in trickery as an artistic mode. "O, but to have gulled him,/ Had been a mastery." In contrast, Face reveals the source of his satisfaction in his work. It lies in calculating his share of the substantial sum of money the firm gained that day.

There is an interesting point that may be missed in the passage where Face describes the part that Dol is to play with the Spaniard. Dol was Subtle's doxy, not Face's. Face speaks the lines which detail, with salacious glee, Dol's seduction of the Spanish don; it is possible that Subtle is not quite as happy at the prospect of her playing the prostitute.

Face's delight carries over into the scene with Drugger and Kastrill. Even as he lies to the stupid and purse-proud Kastrill, a man who would live by his wits but would not gamble, he finds time to bully Drugger. "Hast brought the damask?" "bring the damask." And as Drugger leaves, once again "the damask!" Joyously, he reveals all the secrets of his trade to Kastrill, who cannot see their significance. The doctor, he says correctly, made him a captain just two months back; before that he was a mere pimp. All those who live by their wits are men who have lost their fortunes, and, more daringly "when your land is gone." In effect, he warns Kastrill of their intentions, but Kastrill proceeds blindly and rushes home to bring his sister.

In Kastrill's desire to know the rules for quarreling, Jonson is incidentally satirizing an aspect of manners in his day—the swordsman trained in foreign punctilio. It might be interesting to look at two famous passages in Shakespeare: Mercutio's description of Tybalt, in *Romeo and Juliet,* "a duelist, a duelist" (Act II, Scene 4). And Touchstone's discourse on the causes of quarreling, starting with the "Retort Courteous" and proceeding to the "Lie Direct" (*As You Like It,* Act V, Scene 4). The two dramatists direct different kinds of satire at the same ridiculous code.

At the end of the passage there is again an indication that the partnership must fall apart: "Subtle and I/ Must wrestle for her [i.e., Dame Pliant].

After the departure of the Puritans, the customers start to tumble over each other. Dapper, Drugger, and Kastrill are onstage at the same time, and Sir Epicure arrives before Dapper has been thoroughly diddled.

The treatment of Dapper shows how each client is handled in a fashion proper for him. Neither Mammon nor the Puritans could be put upon by so crude a performance. The approach to Dapper is farcical and completely contemptuous. When Sir Epicure shows up, to the question of what is to be done with Dapper, the answer is "lay him back awhile" like a bag of potatoes. The choice of the privy is simply the final insult. As they rush about the stage, each getting ready to play his next role, changing costumes, shoving the blindfolded Dapper about, they have no feeling that he will sense anything amiss. They are right. He *is* a bag of vegetables.

ACT IV – SCENE 1
(IV – 1-3)

Summary

Face (as Ulen) and Mammon enter; Mammon has come to woo the wealthy lord's sister. Since Subtle presumably knows nothing of this little intrigue, he is busy in his laboratory. Dol plays the gracious and learned lady well, and Sir Epicure greets her courteously; incidentally, he gives her a ring and tips Face generously. Again Sir Epicure engages in one of his fantasies of wealth. Ulen Spiegel interrupts, for other guests are expected, and he suggests that they go to some other part of the house.

Kastrill and his sister have arrived. Before the partners see her, they agree once again to draw lots for her, although each of them intends to cheat the other if he loses. Since Face is still dressed as the servant, he introduces the victims into the room. Subtle, who was not present when Kastrill visited earlier, awes him with a display of learning in the art of quarreling, but his attention is diverted very readily to the widow. Subtle kisses her twice, and toys with her hand, all, of course, in the interest of his science. He is apparently proceeding apace in his wooing when Face, dressed as the captain, enters to tell him that the Spanish don is outside. After Subtle leads Kastrill and his sister to his chamber, he and Face quarrel, for each wants Dame Pliant. Both threaten to reveal their plan to Dol who, presumably, would object to either one's marriage.

The Spanish don, we discover, is Surly in disguise. The conspirators insult him in English to confirm everything Surly suspected. But a problem has arisen: Dol, who was to entertain the Spanish don, is occupied with Sir Epicure, and this man is no

Dapper to be put by until she has completed one chore and is ready to take on another. Face now improvises out of necessity; Dame Pliant is to be substituted for Dol. Suddenly the two conspirators change their attitudes to the lady. Each one wants the other to marry the woman after she has been tricked into playing the whore. Her fortune is still attractive—but not the idea of marriage. Eventually Face agrees that he will marry Dame Pliant, and Surly is led off to his bath.

Summary

The action in the intrigue has accelerated to the point where the conspirators are no longer in complete control. They are frantically trying to juggle the various plots. It is fortunate that they have a large house. Dapper is gagged and blindfolded in the privy; Sir Epicure is wooing Dol in the garden or the great hall, Kastril and Dame Pliant are in the laboratory, the don and Dame Pliant will presumably soon be in some other room. And our heroes are rushing about changing costumes and personalities, playing various parts to various people whom they have to keep apart, and becoming more and more harassed. They have perhaps more prosperity than they can manage.

Sir Epicure plays the gallant well, as Dol plays her part well. In only one passage does Mammon's humour emerge, the description of the sybaritic life they will lead when they are married.

Dame Pliant, as the name indicates, is naive, perhaps stupid, good-natured, easy to convince; Subtle can sway her easily. He is more familiar than good manners sanction in his kissing; he kisses her, then fondles her hand. But then, is he not the privileged great man? This rude familiarity continues under the eye of her brother, who has not wit enough to see. Nor does she resent it. She is after all, the pliant widow, and she is even enthusiastic in her praise. "Brother,/ He's a rare man, believe me!" If Face and Subtle ever resolved their differences and tried to trick her into marriage with one of them, they would succeed, for anyone who would woo her with vigor must succeed.

The contempt for the Spaniard that the conspirators display takes the form of rude insults in English. As the audience well knows, this is a serious error. Surly, of course, plays to the audience. As Face and Subtle talk, he reacts variously with anger which he barely controls, with triumph, or with glee. Only their own confidence, now grown to carelessness, keeps them from noticing.

The battle over who is to marry Dame Pliant has many implications, comic, satiric, and moral. Dame Pliant with her fortune is indeed a prize. Yet both fear Dol's reactions, and both are squeamish about marrying the widow after she is debauched. This niceness of appetite is perhaps the ultimate hypocrisy on the part of those who exploit the hypocrisy of others.

ACT IV – SCENE 2
(IV – 4)

Summary

The two conspirators proceed about their business. Dame Pliant's horoscope reveals that she is to marry a Spanish count, far more desirable than a mere English count. Dame Pliant has an understandable English prejudice against her homeland's traditional enemy, but, as her name indicates, she is easily convinced. After some byplay, for she must make the first overtures (the prostitute, which the don believes her to be, would not be bashful), she and the count leave the room together. Subtle and Kastrill go off for lessons in the fine art of quarreling.

Commentary

This scene advances the plot, but the mark of the great or simply successful comic writer is that no scene merely advances the plot. The important elements of comic action in this scene are two. One is the facile improvisation as the scoundrels bully Dame Pliant. The other is not so immediately apparent on reading. Surly pretends to believe that the lady is a prostitute; the two men strive to keep him in that opinion, while pretending to Dame Pliant that his behavior is the normal manner of a Spanish gentleman when courting a virtuous lady. To maintain the double lie on the stage involves energy and ingenuity. By the time the count and Dame Pliant have left the stage, Subtle and Face are a pair of exhausted plotters.

ACT IV – SCENE 3
(IV – 3)

Summary

The conversation between Sir Epicure and Dol has run into trouble. The knight triggered Dol's madness by mentioning the "Fifth Monarchy," an item of theological controversy. She is spouting odds and ends of theology while Sir Epicure runs about helplessly trying to soothe her fit. Face (now dressed as Ulen) enters in perturbation, for presumably Subtle does not know that Mammon has met the mad sister of a lord.

When Subtle enters, he is again the holy practitioner, horrified by what he sees. He can only interpret Dol's fit of madness as the result of an attempt to hide some immoral activity—"close deeds of darkness." This he says is the reason things have not been proceeding well in the laboratory. Sir Epicure is overcome with remorse; his purpose was chaste. Ulen, he insists further, is blameless, for he (Mammon) persuaded Ulen to help him woo the lady after he saw her accidentally. In any case, says Subtle, the work will be held up a month at least. At this moment there is an explosion offstage. Face enters to announce that all the "work" is destroyed, and Subtle faints. Since there is knocking at the door, Face tells Mammon this is the girl's brother. Mammon is convinced that the fault is all his—"curst fruits," as Subtle says, "of vice and lust!"

Subtle is relieved that one of the projects is ended. Now they must return to the don, who should, by now, have seduced the all too pliant Dame. Subtle cannot resist commenting on the fact that Face is now to marry the be-whored widow.

Commentary

This scene is obvious farce. Dol rushes about in pretended madness, followed by an awkward Sir Epicure. Face, not yet completely dressed as Ulen, joins in buffeting the bewildered knight about, to make sure that he does not quiet Dol. Dol's madness becomes the comic excuse for destroying all the alchemical work; yet, even as Face bundles Sir Epicure out of the house, he manages to get another 100 pounds. Sir Epicure agrees that he will give 100 pounds to the box at Bethlehem, as penance. Face rises to the occasion, "I'll send one to you to receive it." Such devoted attention to business is praiseworthy.

The implications of Mammon's behavior are interesting and not entirely obvious. His acceptance of blame indicates how completely he has been gulled. Although concupiscence formed part of Mammon's motives, he courted Dol, not to despoil her, but to make a socially desirable match. He can see that the same grasping desire for wealth and power that led to his quest of the stone is now the cause of his downfall. His gulling is complete; he has accepted his failure as a product of his own nature, and at the very end he can still be cozened of another 100 pounds. In their designs upon him, the swindlers found that Mammon was himself their greatest ally.

ACT IV – SCENE 4
(IV – 6-7)

Summary

The plan to serve the Spanish don and debauch Dame Pliant has not been proceeding as anticipated. Surly has revealed himself to the lady and is pleading his case in marriage, honestly admitting his poverty and depending on her gratitude. When Subtle enters and tries to pick his pocket, Surly throws off his disguise. Face runs out of the room and returns with Kastrill, who is so anxious to test his new skill in quarreling that he cannot listen when his sister tries to tell what she has learned. Drugger enters to add his bit (incidentally, bringing the damask), testifying, quite honestly, that Surly is a poor man, and his debtor for tobacco, lotion, and syringes. When Ananias enters to inform Subtle that the congregation has decided that "casting of dollars is concluded lawful," Subtle enlists his efforts against Surly, the man in "Spanish slops." Ananias rises to the bait eagerly, for Catholic Spain is the great enemy. Outnumbered five to one, Surly now can only make his escape.

Face gets rid of his allies rapidly. Kastrill has quarreled bravely; Face tells him to follow Surly. He whispers to Drugger, that he, the tobacconist, was to have wooed the widow. So Drugger is off to rent a Spanish suit from the actors. Subtle tells Ananias that they will be happy to cast dollars, but it will have to be in some other spot, for fear of the police. Face now tries to raise the spirits of the shaken Subtle, who "is so down upon the least disaster!" They have, after all, survived the crisis! Subtle revives enough to argue that, since Dame Pliant's virtue is preserved, the matter of her disposition should be renegotiated.

But a new crisis has arisen, one that will be harder to resolve: Dol announces that the master of the house has come. Outside the door is Lovewit surrounded by forty neighbors! Face has to be shaved, to look again like Jeremy, the butler. Subtle and Dol are to escape with what goods they can; Face will greet his master now, but the confederacy is to meet the next day to divide the spoils at an appointed rendezvous.

Commentary

Life is a little too full for the swindlers; they have too many balls to juggle. Yet, when the house of cards falls about them, it is not due to a lack of ingenuity on the part of the manipulators. They showed great ingenuity when they routed Surly in a brilliant coup; Surly, after all, should have defeated them ignominiously. The arrival of Lovewit was not something they could control.

It is noteworthy that Jonson brings Ananias onstage, but not Tribulation. Ananias rises in wrath at the sight of the Spanish dress. Tribulation is the more avaricious of the two, gullible because he is avaricious, but not as naive as Ananias.

The staging emphasizes the comedy of the growing mob of fools who surround Surly, and their subsequent rapid departure as the conspirators get rid of them.

A small point: the exit of Dame Pliant is not noted by a stage direction (in any of the editions examined). It would presumably occur when Kastrill says "Away, you talk like a foolish mauther."

ACT V – SCENE 1
(V – 1-3)

Summary

Outside the house, the neighbors eagerly tell Lovewit of the mysterious activities during his absence. He wonders about skulduggery but thinks only in terms of normal swindles—freak shows, dentistry, or bawdy puppet plays. When Face appears, now clean shaven and back in his full-time role of Jeremy, the butler, he denies everything. He has been alone in the house, with only the cat, who unfortunately caught the plague. For more than three weeks "the door has not been opened." When the neighbors begin to modify their stories, Lovewit assumes that they were lying completely.

Unfortunately, the victims now begin to arrive—first Surly and Mammon; Surly recognizes Jeremy as Captain Face, and he and Mammon leave to fetch the constable. Kastrill and the Puritans arrive, and they too go off for the constable. But Lovewit is bewildered and still believes Jeremy; when the neighbors recognize some of the people they have seen going in and out of the house, Lovewit feels that the good folk have switched stories again.

The trap is sprung, however, when Dapper, whom Subtle and Face have forgotten in the excitement, calls from inside. He has finally eaten his way through the gingerbread gag. When

Lovewit sees Face trying to talk to someone in the house, Face admits that trickery had been in progress. He hopes for forgiveness, however, because he will be able to help Lovewit to a young, beautiful, and wealthy wife. But he suggests they enter the house so that he can describe the events in private.

Commentary

The arrival of Lovewit is a *deus ex machina*, literally a "god out of the machine," an improbable character suddenly introduced by the author to resolve the action. When Lovewit, barely mentioned before, arrives it is certain that the intrigues will collapse, if only because the fifth act has been reached. But Face still wrestles nobly, trying to forestall ruin. If it were not for Dapper, he would overcome his victims once again.

Most modern readers find the belated introduction of Lovewit unsatisfactory. Although we cannot be certain, we can speculate on Jonson's reasons for resolving the play in this way.

1. It is likely that he could not permit any of the gulls to overcome. There is no one that arouses either respect or affection; they are as guilty of avarice and hypocrisy as the conspirators. The outsider is therefore necessary.

2. Surly has an intensity about him that Jonson does not approve. He is not balanced; he is in his own way a fanatic.

3. Lovewit, while hardly drawn to our complete satisfaction, represents a type which Jonson liked. "I love a teeming wit," says Lovewit, "as I love my nourishment." And Jeremy says later, "Sir, you were wont to affect mirth and wit." He is an urbane gentleman. He has not, we might believe, the hypocrisy or the single-minded avarice of the school of cullies; he would not be fool enough to be taken in by alchemy, astrology, or palmistry.

Face's asides seem to indicate a conscience become faint for the best of all reasons — his sins are catching up with him.

ACT V – SCENE 2
(V – 4)

Summary

Inside the house business is going on almost as usual; Subtle must deal with Dapper, and Face, again a captain, helps. He has apparently taken care of his master, at least temporarily; Dapper has still to be introduced to the Queen of Fairy. Dol, dressed as the Queen, enters, and after some mystic promises, Dapper is given amulets and is dispatched. Even at this late moment, the cheats are still at work—Dapper is to turn over his estate to the Queen.

But Drugger, who was promised the widow for a wife, has returned with a Spanish robe; Subtle sends him off for the parson. Now Subtle and Dol conspire, for he assumes that Face is planning to marry Dame Pliant, contrary to the rigid agreement of the three swindlers. When Dol and Subtle leave with what spoils they can carry, they will not go to the appointed rendezvous. In the meantime, Dol is to try to swindle Dame Pliant.

When Face returns they pack goods, gloating over their list, until Face springs his surprise: the spoils will never leave now that his master has returned. The best Face can do is permit them to escape as poor and empty-handed as when they first started working together. They are angry, but leave, for what choice have they?

Commentary

Some little time must pass between the first scene and the second. Face has had time to talk to Lovewit, to gain his cooperation, and to don the captain's disguise. Presumably he now wears an obviously false beard, as he has already shaved the one he grew as the captain. Subtle and Dol are as contemptuous as ever in their handling of Dapper. Quite properly. He is once more befuddled, and is sent off to fetch the "writings" to his estate.

The two men are now trying to double-cross each other. As Subtle assumes that Face is preparing to marry Dame Pliant, he and Dol are fully justified in cheating Face of the treasure. Face is playing a more devious game. He has made his peace with his employer, too soon returned. He pretends to be taken in by Subtle and Dol, but the ace of trump is up his sleeve. The law, the establishment, and vested authority are now all on his side. He knows, and regrets, that he will not marry the wealthy widow, but he takes what pleasure he can in out-maneuvering his cheating confederates. He can salve his pride as well as circumstances permit. As his asides in the scene before clearly show, the line, "I sent for him," is a lie. But he can feel he has outwitted somebody.

While there is still another scene, the justice meted out the prime malfactors is complete here. Dol and Subtle entered the confederacy having nothing, "taking their meals in steam." They leave having nothing. Face was Jeremy, the butler, having nothing. Face is again Jeremy, the butler, having nothing, for the widow and the spoils of their efforts are the blackmail he pays Lovewit to forgive and protect him. Lovewit inherits wealth, and a young, beautiful, and wealthy (even though not very intelligent) wife.

ACT V – SCENE 3
(V – 5)

Summary

As the scene opens, Lovewit appears wearing the Spanish costume in which he married Dame Pliant. The marriage is presumably consummated ("Is it a marriage? perfect?"). But now the house is besieged by the screaming victims, accompanied by a constable carrying a warrant. Lovewit's story is ready. Jeremy has admitted that he leased the house to a doctor and a captain while Lovewit was away. In fact, they caused much damage – the walls of one room are ruined by exploding chemicals. The only person he found was one gentlewoman, and since she was waiting to marry a Spanish count who apparently deserted her, he Lovewit, married her. When Mammon finds his goods in the basement, and wants to salvage them, Lovewit is quite willing, if Mammon brings a court order. To get it, the knight would have to explain how he was cheated of his property. The price is, it seems, a little too high, and Mammon and Surly leave. Ananias and Tribulation also feel they have claim to the goods, for they bought them. To them Lovewit is not even polite. Drugger he scares away, and Jeremy sends the parson to tell Drugger that he could meet the doctor and the captain in some weird far-off places.

This leaves Kastrill, angry that his sister has not married a lord and eager to quarrel. But Mammon "quarrels" first, and Kastrill, cowed in the very art he so admires, is won over—"'Slight, I must love him!" For Lovewit, the recipient of the fruits of others' toil, married to a beautiful, wealthy, and compliant wife, truly all's well.

Face addresses the audience graciously, and the play ends.

Commentary

Although the introduction of Lovewit as a way to resolve the action seems a makeshift to us, there is nothing haphazard about the play once he is introduced. The gulls do not quietly withdraw; Lovewit (or Jonson) motivates their withdrawal in accordance with their characters.

Dame Pliant presents no problem. She has accepted the change of events, and now, wedded and bedded, is ripely fulfilled. She either knows by now that her Spanish count is an English gentleman, or she will discover it shortly. This will doubtless please her too; she gained some audience goodwill earlier when she said that she did not like the Spanish.

Surly is shocked to hear of the marriage. He is one of the two characters whose handling presents an ethical problem (Lovewit is the other). Why should he, the honest man, not have been rewarded? How Jonson saw him is made clear in this scene.

His claim to Dame Pliant's hand and fortune, advanced earlier, was based on the fact that he was completely honest with her and spared her the indignity of debauchery. In the character of Surly, Jonson substituted for the obvious sins of the others a different kind of sin. Surly assumed intelligence and gratitude in people. The virtue in which he prided himself, that he did not debauch Dame Pliant, was a mistake. Surly, has after all some of the Puritan about him; he is the Malcontent. Lovewit has prospered, for he is at peace in the world and at home in his own skin. Surly can well say "I needs cheat myself/ With that same foolish vice of honesty!"

Mammon is more than merely gulled. As Lovewit shrewdly adduces, he "did cozen himself." In a moment he has convinced himself that "the Commonwealth" has sustained a loss; and more honestly, before he leaves: "I will... preach/ The end of the world within these two months." Self-delusion is a way of life for him. We would not be surprised if he and Subtle do business together again one day.

The treatment of Tribulation and Ananias may surprise us a little. They did buy metal articles (even if they were not Subtle's to sell), but they are dispatched without explanation. The contempt that Lovewit and Jonson both feel for the Puritans is too strong to allow either to treat them with any politeness. Drugger, of course, is no problem. Lovewit says "boo" and he runs.

The handling of Kastrill is an excellent stroke. He is outquarreled by Lovewit, to whom the art of quarreling like a gentleman comes naturally, and Kastrill admires the victor. His brother-in-law is not a lord, but he is more; he is Kastrill's ideal: he can quarrel, smoke, and drink. The young man is happy to add 500 pounds to his sister's portion.

A line in Face's last speech is significant. "My part a little fell in this last scene,/ Yet 'twas decorum." The aspect of decorum emphasized here is the decorum of class. Lovewit is present; therefore he has taken over the conduct of affairs. The butler has moved into the background.

CHARACTERIZATION

There is a certain irreducible minimum of characterization in any play. Plays exist where the playwright gave no thought to creating characters, but simply supplied lines that the actors would speak to unfold the plot. There are still "characters," supplied by the actors and by the tendency of the audience to establish a consistent pattern. Successful characterization, however, demands a considerable effort that great dramatists are willing to supply.

Since the character has to be convincing to the viewers, the dramatist must take into account values that are acceptable to his audience. These values are not always universal or timeless, and the certainty of one age is sometimes the farce of another. Jonson based his characterization on two considerations that formed part of the texture of the attitude to life in his day. The first we might think of as an ethical need of his audience, the second as an Elizabethan system of psychology.

The ethical need involved the distribution of fitting reward or punishment. Toward the end of the century, the acidulous critic, Thomas Rymer, gave to this concept the name "poetic justice." By poetic justice he meant a kind of justice whereby the punishment fit the crime; and the characters received their just deserts by the end of the play. While the doctrine can be dangerous in the interpretation of tragedy, it is very useful when applied to comedy.

In the kind of comedy we know best, the fate of the character at the end of the play must always satisfy the viewer's sense of right and wrong. Now, the relationship between character and plot can be looked at from either end. We may say that if the character is created in a particular way, then the play must have a certain conclusion; or, we may say that, if the plot is designed to show the eventual downfall of a character, *then* the character must be created so that his downfall is appropriate. It is likely that, as Jonson wrote the play, the sense of character and sense of plot were both operating at the same time. Although Jonson's handling of some characters creates problems for us, there is no doubt that he felt he was meting out proper retribution for the characters. They are created in ethical terms. We can think of them as *deserving* or *undeserving*.

Related closely to this ethical control, is the fact that characters in this play also form a satiric spectrum of London social types. To fulfill the requirements of the satire, they must also be properly punished. As satiric examples, they are on the whole, unchanging. Jonson, in fact, makes the point in the play that they do not learn from their experiences.

Every age has its own theory or theories of personality, its own psychology. In our age, for instance, we are likely to think of people's characters as molded by stresses due to family ties or to the pressures of society. Jonson's theory of personality was generally, although not universally, accepted by the Renaissance.

The doctrine of humours is derived from the Middle Ages and earlier. According to this doctrine, the body consisted of four humours (or moistures), blood, phlegm, yellow bile (choler), and black bile (melancholy). When these were in proportion within the individual, he was healthy. Jonson wrote two comedies, *Every Man in His Humour* and *Every Man out of His Humour*, where he relied, presumably completely, on the doctrine of humours as a basis for his characters' personalities. Such an approach constituted a scientific justification for the extreme character types that have always been a staple of comedy.

Jonson stated his position in the opening scene of *Every Man out of His Humour* and the key lines are worth quoting.

> ... so in every human body
> The choler, melancholy, phlegm, and blood,

> By reason that they flow continually
> In some one part, and are not continent,
> Receive the name of humours. Now thus far
> It may, by metaphor, apply itself
> Unto the general disposition:
> As when some one peculiar quality
> Doth so possess a man, that it doth draw
> All his affects, his spirits, and his powers,
> In their confluctions, all to run one way,
> This may be truly said to be a humour.

However, humours were not as important in Jonson's later plays. In the twelve years between *Every Man in His Humour* (1598) and *The Alchemist* (1610) his emphasis shifted. *The Alchemist,* like *Volpone* a few years earlier, was a satiric attack on the moral faults, greed and hypocrisy. In *The Alchemist* "humour" means simply a quirk of character. Surly says, "I have a humour,/ I would not willingly be gulled," i.e., "I have an odd quirk of character. I do not like to be cheated."

Tied to these broad principles of character creation are two devices that can be considered points of craftsmanship. Jonson always supplied a thorough introduction for each character on his first appearance. We know Subtle, Face, Dol in the first scene. We also know each of the victims as he arrives. We even know Lovewit, for the key information is given us at once. After their introduction, characters do not develop during the play.

The other device is the language. The dramatic verse is discussed elsewhere, and any examination of the poetry must include a study of language and images. But language and images are also as important for characterization as the ideas or informational content of speeches. Jonson strives for, and, in some cases, achieves magnificent effects. Subtle, for instance, obviously talks about alchemy. That is necessary for him and for the plot of the play. But Subtle, we can see, *thinks* in terms of alchemy. He boasts of the help he has been to Face by saying he has, "sublimed" him, "exalted" him, and "fixed" him in "the third region" "wrought" him "to spirit, to quintessence": all metaphors drawn from alchemy. In every word Mammon reveals his dreams, his preoccupation with fantasies of grandeur, sybaritic luxury, and food. The Puritans are equally obvious. They talk the jargon of the Puritans (as Jonson sees them) at every moment. Ananias introduces himself as a "servant" of the exiled "brethren," and he reports to "the Saints." Were the orphans "sincere professors"? This preoccupation with language forms a pattern whereby the participants are characterized and satirized.

REVIEW QUESTIONS

1. Discuss *The Alchemist* as a treatment of the themes of (a) avarice, (b) hypocrisy, and (c) self-delusion.

2. Compare and contrast the following pairs of characters: (a) Subtle and Face, (b) Surly and Lovewit.

3. The victims can be divided into the fools and the knaves. Discuss them on this basis.

4. Discuss the importance in this play, of (a) alchemy, (b) magic.

5. Consider the propriety of rewards and punishments in this play.

6. Compare the satire in *The Alchemist* with Jonson's *Volpone*.

7. Discuss farce in *The Alchemist*.

8. Discuss the propriety of the names given characters in the play.

NOTES

NOTES

NOTES

NOTES